the black self

the

black self

marvin d. wyne,
kinnard p. white,
richard h. coop
University of North Carolina

PRENTICE-HALL, INC., ENGLEWOOD CLIFFS, NEW JERSEY

Library of Congress Cataloging in Publication Data

WYNE, MARVIN D.
    The Black self.

    Includes bibliographies.
        1. Negroes—Race identity.   2. Negroes—Psychology.
I. White, Kinnard P., joint author.   II. Coop, Richard
H., joint author.   III. Title.
E185.625W95 1974   155.8'4'96073   74-1415
ISBN 0-13-077420-0
ISBN 0-13-077412-X (pbk.)

PRINTED IN THE UNITED STATES OF AMERICA

10   9   8   7   6   5   4   3   2   1

PRENTICE-HALL INTERNATIONAL, INC., London
PRENTICE-HALL OF AUSTRALIA, PTY. LTD., Sydney
PRENTICE-HALL OF CANADA, LTD., Toronto
PRENTICE-HALL OF INDIA PRIVATE LIMITED, New Delhi
PRENTICE-HALL OF JAPAN, INC., Tokyo

to
Martin Luther King, Jr.
and
The Realization of His Dream

contents

3

PERSONAL CONTROL AND THE BLACK SELF   45

4

THE SOCIAL CONTEXT OF THE BLACK SELF   63

5
THE FUTURE OF THE BLACK SELF   83

preface

Robert Coles (1967) relates a conversation he shared with an elderly black woman whose family was one of many currently embroiled in a school integration battle. When Coles asked if she believed the problems of Negroes were in any way similar to problems faced by white people, this was her answer:

> "Yes, we is all the same under God, so we has the same problems, but colored folk has special ones, too. It's the same being colored as white, but it's different being colored, too."
> Then she repeated, as though to emphasize the words, "It's the same, but it's different." (p. 255.)

Coles used the profound simplicity of her answer to remind researchers that there are serious dangers associated with observing, studying, and describing people on the basis of their race, as if all human beings did not share much more than they hold exclusive.

It is to the samenesses and the differences that this book on the black self is directed. Its purpose is to bring together theory and research related to the self-concepts of black Americans. *The Black Self* is addressed to human-relations groups and college courses in educational psychology, sociology, human growth and development, special education, guidance and coun-seling, and student teaching.

This book illustrates the contingencies under which the black self is formed and illuminates the effects of those contingencies on black American behavioral patterns. Numerous texts and research articles have been written on self-concept, but very little attention has been given to research or theory regarding the development of self in black Americans. There is still more fallacy than fact and more heat than light surrounding self-perceptions of black individuals. A concomitant role of *The Black Self* is to stimulate research interest in this crucial developmental construct which is bound to an undeniable history of prejudice and discrimination.

M.D.W.
K.P.W.
R.H.C.

Chapel Hill, North Carolina

the black self

1

self-image:
a concept in search of
a theory

Self is the only prison that can ever bind the soul.

Henry Van Dyke, "The Prison and the Angel"

The people that walked in darkness have seen a great light.

Isaiah 9:2

Historical and Theoretical Development of
Self-Concept

Behavioral scientists cannot specify precisely when the child acquires a concept of self, but they can identify many of the crucial factors in the child's environment which influence, positively or negatively, his self-concept. Generally speaking, this book is about the relationship between the individual and his total environment. Specifically, the remainder of this chapter and those which follow focus on the self-image of black American children and young adults.

Some may question whether self-concept of black children and youth is sufficiently different from the study of self in other groups to justify separate examination. *The fact that the self-image of black Americans is fundamentally related to a color-caste system justifies exclusive treatment of the topic.* From the very beginning of this country's history, blacks have been relegated to a position inferior to whites. Some colonies objected to early drafts of the Declaration of Independence, because these drafts included a clause which took issue with the imposition of Negro slavery upon America by England. That clause did not appear in the final version which was accepted. The present color-caste system in the United States grew out of attempts to explain away the owning, trading, and selling of Negro slaves.

It is difficult to imagine how the personality and self-concept of the black American could fail to be influenced by the experience of caste discrimination based solely upon his skin color. There is a wealth of evidence to support the contention that one of the first social evidences a black child receives concerning his self-image has to do with the color of his skin (Clark & Clark, 1939, 1940, 1950; Dai, 1956; Kardiner & Ovesey, 1962; Brody, 1963, 1964; Rainwater, 1966; Coles, 1967).

The current state of knowledge about the source and the effects of the black self-image is fraught with confusion and contradiction. However, one fact emerges clearly from the mosaic of theory, speculation, and information—there is a unique blend of biological, psychological, and sociological conditions which combine to form *the* black self-concept. This does not mean that self-concept among black Americans does not show many variations across age, sex, socioeconomic status, and geographic region—indeed it does. Positing the notion that *the* black self-concept exists does mean, however, that blacks develop self-images which are peculiar to the conditions associated with their culture in twentieth-century America. Despite the sadly shortsighted attempts of whites "not to notice," black Americans are culturally different people who are not and never have been fully accepted in the mainstream of this nation's life. Heady statements about cultural pluralism notwithstanding, the Americanized black individual has experienced a long history of oppression, both obvious and subtle, profoundly affecting the image he develops of himself as a person. C. Franklin Edwards (1966) observed that the fears, suspicions, and feelings of inadequacy generated in the black man by his subordinate status are not to be found in the experiences of immigrant groups, for example. Further, skin color and other clearly distinguishable physical traits separate blacks from other groups in the society. These unique characteristics have been taken as physical stigmata which tend to reinforce negative attitudes toward the black American. Edwards suggests that "...the attitudes of the Negro toward himself are merely reciprocals of the attitudes of other groups toward him" (p. 282).

Difficulties in Objective Study of Black Self-Concept

We are aware of the problems involved in separating ethnic factors and socioeconomic variables in studies of black self-concept—race and socioeconomic status overlap and interact in an inseparable blend of confusion and misunderstanding.

It must be understood that the amalgam of behaviors and conditions created by the interaction of *ethnic group membership and socioeconomic position* profoundly affects the objective study of either. The interaction between the individual self and the environment which shapes it becomes very complicated when there is no single, simple pattern to follow, but rather, numerous subcultural variants operating simultaneously. The social scientists' data can be "poisoned" and his ultimate conclusions weakened or distorted by taking the urban ghetto black individual out of context. There is a variety of "minicultures" operating within any subculture. The further we attempt to reduce the influence of ethnic group membership on individual behavior, the more crucial objective precision becomes. At this point, the writer usually tosses a scholarly crumb toward scientific method by exclaiming that he will "consider these factors (socioeconomic position, region, ethnic group, age, sex) one by one"; and that *he* (although he usually says *we*) "must not forget that these factors are inextricably bound together in their interaction within the individual."

Simply recognizing the complex and dynamic nature of this interaction does not make it go away. It certainly does not excuse the web of fiction woven from cause-effect statements and the unwarranted conclusions which sometimes follow. Place yourself in the position of the scientist-scholar-writer who is honestly attempting to grapple with this problem. You are trying to solve a jigsaw puzzle, the pieces varying in size, shape, and color. Each piece has been given a label—the larger pieces are called ethnic group, sex, color, socioeconomic status, age, values; other pieces have names like unemployment, attitude, child-rearing, crime, mental illness, delinquency, dropout, illegitimacy, hostility, and so on. You find it necessary to examine each piece separately in order to determine its contribution to the total puzzle—so far, so good! As you refer to the puzzle picture on the front of the box (assuming a complete picture is available, which of course it is not), you notice that the picture is slowly changing. You are dismayed to realize that the puzzle pieces you are studying no longer fit neatly, if indeed, they ever did. Next, consider what happens when you turn to the "puzzle experts" for help. Each expert (physician, psychiatrist, educator, social worker, welfare caseworker, legal aid representative, parole officer, economic opportunity or poverty program worker) jealously claims certain pieces; other pieces fought over as staked-out claims are continuously jumped and disputed.

We readily admit the oversimplified nature of the analogy, and we do not present it to excuse our attempt to explain maladjustment. Conditions in the United States demand solutions to the social and economic problems which are rooted in the booming, whirling confusion of the factors listed above. The catalyst for these solutions ultimately resides in the individual.

Those studies which have attempted to determine the unique contributions of each of these factors (ethnic group membership and socioeconomic status) have indicated that ethnic group membership does play a crucial role in the development of self. Further, there is evidence from interview data that both blacks and whites believe that ethnic group membership is important (Pettigrew, 1964). More studies linking lower-class blacks and poor self-image are not needed. We are already painfully aware of this interaction. Discovering those features of the environment which relate to the individual's self-concept should receive highest priority. The stress of this book will be to concentrate on these aspects of the black condition that seem to influence self-concept.

Much more will be said (Chapter 2) about the conditions associated with the formation of self-images in black Americans. Our purpose is to reveal the sets of circumstances which are most likely to result in positive and negative self-attitudes. More important, our objective is to provide increased understanding of how and why these circumstances have the influences they do and what can realistically be done about them.

One variable, in particular, seems to be of such crucial significance in the development of self-concepts among black Americans that it has been set forth in a separate chapter (Chapter 3). This variable is most often referred to by psychologists as "locus of control" and by sociologists as "alienation." An eloquent and powerful description of the importance of the amount and type of control which many black Americans feel over their lives is presented by Rainwater (1966). He holds that the black lower-class family is the "crucible of identity" for the child in a manner quite distinct from that of the families of children of other cultural groups.

It seems likely that one of the advantages of being reared in a family setting which creates a stable, relatively predictable psychosocial environment is that such an environment should foster the development of a greater degree of emotional independence and inner control. If a child finds little in his unstable past to help him adapt to present situations and little in his present conditions to encourage looking toward and planning for the future, it should not be surprising to find that he perceives his life to be largely externally controlled. Bernstein (1961) described lower-class family settings as less formally organized than middle-class families in relation to the development of the child.

> Although the authority within the family is explicit, the values which it expresses do not give rise to the carefully ordered universe spatially and temporally of the middle class child. The exercise of authority will not be related to a stable system of rewards and punishments but may often appear arbitrary. The specific character of long-term goals tends to be replaced by more general notions of the future, in which chance, a friend or a relative plays a greater part than the rigorous working out of connections (p. 162).

Such an environment doubtlessly has negative effects on the perception the developing child has of his ability to influence his own life and life chances. If lower-class black children do perceive themselves as externally controlled, it may be that Erikson's (1966) notions about identity formation in black children and youth have some validity. These children may not "develop" self-images; it may be more nearly proper to speak of their "adopting" self-images.

Historical Development of Self

Man's insatiable curiosity about himself is at least as old as his recorded history. He has used words such as spirit, soul, mind, psyche, proprium, and being to refer to his selfhood. The mystery of his creation, purpose, death, and his ultimate future is reflected in man's philosophy and in his theology. Interest in human behavior resulted in the development of the science of psychology. Perhaps because psychology was one of the last to leave the womb of the mother science—philosophy—it has been particularly subject to the influences of the ideological split between rationalism and empiricism. Philosophical debates between rationalists, such as Descartes, and empiricists, such as Locke, may seem long ago and far away, but the impact of these philosophical doctrines upon modern psychology is quite real and of great importance. The serious scholar of self-concept should study the historical review presented by Diggory (1966, pp. 1-68), which views the study of self-concept in the perspective of the many historically important notions that have contributed to its current status.

Despite great advances in the study of human behavior, self remains an elusive phenomenon, largely because it cannot be directly observed. Self-concept is postulated from observed events on which inferences are based and, as is the case with any construct that must be studied by indirect inference, there has been a tendency to reify the self-concept. Consequently, in practice, self-concept is frequently viewed as if it were a real, observable phenomenon. Self is nothing more than a construct or an idea, which permits the linking of unobservable processes with observable, measurable behavior. Self-concept is only a mechanism which permits behavior to be explained.

The essence of self is feeling. William James (1890) regarded man's belief that he can feel himself thinking and that he distinguishes this mental state as an inward activity separate from all the objects with which it deals as "the most fundamental of all the postulates of Psychology." Freud's theoretical notion concerning man's private feelings about self was referred to as ego. Although Freud did not dwell on self as a central theme, his important theoretical contributions in the area have been greatly expanded by more recent writers (Sullivan, 1947; Mead, 1934; Lewin, 1935; and Goldstein, 1939). Also, the study of the human personality depends to a large extent upon the notion of self-concept. The work of such major personality theorists as Maslow (1954, 1956) and Gordon Allport (1937, 1943, 1955, 1966) particularly depended upon the assumption that self-concept is the core of human personality. Other personality theorists (Snygg & Combs, 1949; Rogers, 1951; and Ausubel, 1952) have advanced the notion that all human behavior is motivated by the drive to maintain and enhance self.

The fundamental importance of self-concept to the study of human behavior is well established. Nevertheless, as the above discussion has indicated, self-concept, despite the greatly increased attention now paid it by behavioral scientists, still remains enigmatic.

Self-Concept Theories

The theoretical development of self-concept is not as easy to outline as its history. Yet, an important reason for the lack of theoretical consistency of self-image actually lies in its history. Wylie (1961) revealed in her review that during the 1920s through the 1940s, the study of self-concept received no systematic attention from American psychology. This dynamic, pubescent period of the growth of psychology was primarily committed to behaviorism and refused to recognize any construct studied only by indirect inference. Consequently, during this period, self-concept was not viewed as a viable psychological construct. Even those who fought for more emphasis on self-image (Mead, 1934, Lewin, 1935, G. Allport, 1937, are salient examples) weakened their own position, because their research could not face up to the strict experimental standards set by the behaviorists.

This long period of negligible research effort accounts in part for the current state of apparent theoretical retardation surrounding self-image. A superficial search of self-concept literature quickly reveals the diverse range of attempts to describe, define, and measure self. It is essentially up to each new entrant into the fray to conceptualize self anew. We have not offered "our" definition of self-concept and, in fact, terms such as self-concept, self-esteem, self-image, and self-identity have been and will be used interchangeably throughout the book. Although some may interpret this eclectic position as a kind of academic "cop-out," others will see it as an honest attempt to reflect the present theoretical complexity and confusion concerning self.

In spite of the inadequate theoretical development of self-concept, several points of common agreement have begun to emerge. First, there is general acceptance of the assumption that self-concept is learned. Second, most of the research on self-concept has revolved around a single dimension—the good-bad or positive-negative dimension (McCandless, 1967, p. 255). Third, self-concept is viewed as being comprised of many different aspects of the person. Although these different aspects or characteristics of the person have been described in many different ways by a large number of authors, there is agreement that self-concept includes the picture the individual has of the appearance of his body; the image he has of how others see him; the feelings he has about himself, his family, and his immediate environment; his feelings of worth or unworthiness, acceptance or rejection; his abilities, skills, and limitations (Jersild, 1952). Fourth, there is general agreement that important relationships exist between self-concept and overall personality. Fifth, there is increasing evidence that self-concept is significantly related to other learnings that the individual must master if he is to adjust to the tasks demanded by society. Purkey (1970), for example, in his concisely written and well-documented synthesis of the research on self-concept and school achievement, concludes that a strong reciprocal relationship exists between these two variables.

We turn now to the problems of defining and measuring self-concept. Definitional problems, the dearth of conceptual models, and inadequate, poorly constructed theories of self have not prevented attempts to measure self-concept, often "in weird and wonderful ways" (McCandless, 1967).

Attempts to Define and Measure Self-Concept

Definitions of self-concept abound. Wylie (1961) and McCandless (1967) have written scholarly reviews of the definitional morass which continues to surround self-concept. The abstract nature of self-concept, while adding to its mystique and consequent wide interest, creates no small amount of confusion as to how self-concept can and should be defined. The importance of definitions for the development of scientific knowledge cannot be overemphasized. Without clear and unequivocal definitions of the intentional meaning of a concept, it is impossible to develop adequate measures of that concept. Adequate measures are an obvious and necessary condition for the development of reliable knowledge about a concept. Although systematic measurement is essential to the development of knowledge, pseudomeasurement of a phenomenon often lends a false scientific aura to that phenomenon. It is, however, in the search for more valid and reliable measuring devices that scientists hope to conceptualize and define more accurately that which they seek to measure. This hope often proves to be empty.

There are some interesting developmental parallels between the constructs of *self-concept* and *intelligence* which may assist in understanding both. These two notions have always been at the center of popular concern, yet the confusion about their nature is still with us. Attempts to formulate a theoretical definition of intelligence which would be generally accepted reached their peak quite early in this century. Yet, with the exception of J. P. Guilford's extension of the early multifactor work, only Piaget has provided truly original progress in our understanding of intelligence since the 1920s. Huge manpower testing requirements of the two world wars is usually given as the primary reason for circumventing further work on the theory of intelligence and for exploding the measurement of intelligence into the monster that we have come to use and accept. No single measure of self-concept has clearly emerged and dominated as the Binet test has in the intelligence-testing movement, and measurement of self-concept lags far behind, although on an apparently parallel path. Despite its questionable theoretical pedigree, the measurement of intelligence is a widely accepted area of behavioral science, and its bastard child, the IQ, has become a badge of distinction for some and a source of shame for others—all of this without a basic understanding of what intelligence is. If we are to develop an understanding of the meaning of self-concept, the study of its theoretical nature must not be forsaken for its assumed practical use.

There are several critical reviews of self-concept measurement to which the interested student may turn (Strong & Feder, 1961; Combs, Courson, & Soper, 1963; Heilbrun, 1965; McCandless, 1967). The basic conclusion of these reviewers is that attempts to measure self-concept have pushed ahead of the development of theoretical rationales, conceptual models, and adequate definitions of self-concept. There have been few persons interested in self-concept theory as it relates to the problem of measurement. As a result, self-concept measures tend to be investigator-and test-specific. Each researcher develops his own measure of self-concept, which is unique to his point of view and which usually relates only vaguely to the broader problems of self-concept. This state of affairs in the measurement of self-concept has largely precluded the development of precise communication among researchers and theorists concerning self. One consequence of this situation is that many researchers use measures of self-concept with the apparent assumption that the various instruments are all measuring the same thing. Although some of these measures may, in fact, approach equivalence, there is considerable evidence that many of them, although sporting the same title, do not measure the same construct.

Combs and Soper (1957) argue cogently that studies which claim to investigate self-concept are actually studies of self-report. They define self-report as "a description of self reported to an outsider" (p. 494). There is a widely accepted assumption that a close relationship exists between what the person reports about his self-concept and his actual self-concept, but this relationship is not one to one. Combs and Soper point out some of the factors that determine how closely self-report approximates the individual's "real" self-concept:

1. The clarity of the individual's awareness.
2. The availability of adequate symbols for expression.
3. The willingness of the individual to cooperate.
4. The social expectancy.

5.   The individual's feeling of personal adequacy.
6.   His feeling of freedom from threat (p. 494).

Gordon's (1966) discussion of measuring self-concept in young children is particularly helpful because of the scarcity of studies of self-concept at early ages. Gordon takes the position that the debate over which self-concept measures are better is pointless. The validity of any self-measuring device should be determined by its usefulness as a predictor of behavior. Furthermore, the primary concern in self-measurement should not be with what the "real self" is but rather with how the individual perceives himself, since reality is not necessarily a determinant of an individual's self-concept.

Although the problems and difficulties of self-measurement are many in number and complex in nature, it is only by objectively analyzing these problems that more precise instruments for measuring self-concept can be developed. Actually, few researchers of self-concept have devoted their energies to the development of valid and theoretically sound measurement instruments. It is important that practitioners be clearly aware of the imperfect nature of self-concept measures if they are to use self-concept data effectively. It is equally important for the helping professional to utilize existing techniques of self-measurement with care if he is to help increase his understanding of and sensitivity to the individual with whom he is interacting.

Regardless of the theoretical problems involving the notion of self and the consequent problems associated with the measurement of self-concept, few psychologists and educators would deny that self-concept is the core of each individual's life space and that all experiences that the individual has are influenced by that personal frame of reference.

If an individual's self-concept greatly influences his personal, social, and academic adjustment, then the implications for psychologists, educators, and other helping professionals are clear. We must first discover as many of the antecedent conditions of self-concept as possible. The home and family have always been viewed as important sources of learning self-identity. The black culture as another segment of the crucible of self-image will be discussed later through social, economic, political, and educational frames of reference.

Can our past and present experience as a racially mixed society produce any evidence to refute Jersild's (1960) contention that,

> ...if the reflected appraisals of which the self is made up are mainly derogatory, then the growing child's attitudes toward himself will be mainly derogatory. The child toward whom the predominant attitude of significant persons has been one of hostility, disapproval, and dissatisfaction will tend to view the world in similar terms. He will have difficulty in seeing or learning anything better, and although he may not openly express self-depreciatory attitudes, he has a depreciatory attitude toward others and toward himself (p. 13).

References

Allport, G. *Personality: A psychological interpretation.* New York: Holt, Rinehart, & Winston, 1937.

Allport, G. The ego in contemporary psychology. *Psychological Review,* 1943, 50, 451-68.

Allport, G. *Becoming.* New Haven, Connecticut: Yale University Press, 1955.

Allport, G. *Pattern and growth in personality.* New York: Holt, Rinehart, & Winston, 1966.

Ausubel, D. *Ego development and the personality disorders.* New York: Grune & Stratton, 1952.

Bernstein, B. Social class and linguistic development: A theory of social learning. In A. Halsey, J. Floud, & C. Anderson (eds.) *Economy, education, and society.* New York: Free Press, 1961.

Brody, E. Color and identity conflict in young boys. *Psychiatry,* 1963, 2, 188-201.

Brody, E. Color and identity conflict in young boys, II. *Archives of General Psychiatry,* 1964, 10, 354-60.

Clark, K., & M. Clark. The development of consciousness of self and the emergence of racial identification in Negro preschool children. *Journal of Social Psychology,* 1939, 4, 591-99.

Clark, K., & M. Clark. Skin color as a factor in racial identification of Negro preschool children. *Journal of Social Psychology,* 1940, 1, 159-69.

Clark, K., & M. Clark. Emotional factors in racial identification and preference in Negro children. *Journal of Negro Education,* 1950, 19, 341-50.

Coles, R. It's the same, but it's different. In T. Parsons & K. Clark (eds.), *The Negro American.* Boston: Beacon Press, 1966.

Combs, A., & D. Soper. The self, its derivate terms, and research. *Journal of Individual Psychology,* 1957, 13, 135-45.

Combs, A., C. Courson, & D. Soper. The measurement of self-concept and self-report. *Educational and Psychological Measurement,* 1963, 23, 493-500.

Dai, B. Some problems of personality development among Negro children. In C. Kluckhohn, H. Murray, & D. Schneider (eds.), *Personality: In nature, society, and culture.* (2nd ed.) New York: Knopf, 1956.

Diggory, J. *Self-evaluation: Concepts and studies.* New York: John Wiley, 1966.

Edwards, C. F. *The Negro professional class.* New York: Free Press, 1966.

Erikson, E. The concept of identity in race relations: Notes and queries. In T. Parsons & K. Clark (eds.), *The Negro American.*

Goldstein, K. *The organism.* New York: American Book Company, 1939.

Gordon, I. *Studying the child in school.* New York: John Wiley, 1966.

Halsey, A, J. Floud, & C. Anderson (eds.). *Economy, education, and society.* New York: Free Press, 1961.

Heilbrun, A. The social desirability variable: Implications for test reliability and validity. *Educational and Psychological Measurement,* 1965, 25, 745-56.

James, W. *Principles of psychology.* (2 vols.) Magnolia, Mass.: Peter Smith, 1890.

Jersild, A. *In search of self.* New York: Bureau of Publications, Teachers College, Columbia University, 1952.

Jersild, A. *Child psychology.* Englewood Cliffs, N.J.: Prentice-Hall, 1960.

Kardiner, A. & L. Ovesey. *The mark of oppression: Explorations in the personality of the American Negro.* Cleveland: World, 1962. (Paperback)

Kluckhohn C., H. Murray, & D. Schneider (eds.). *Personality: In nature, society, and culture.* (2nd ed.) New York: Knopf, 1956.

Lewin, K. *A dynamic theory of personality.* New York: McGraw-Hill, 1935.

Maslow, A. *Motivation and personality.* New York: Harper & Row, 1954.

Maslow, A. Personality problems and personality growth. In C. Moustakas (ed.), *Explorations in personal growth.* New York: Harper & Row, 1956.

McCandless, B. *Children: Behavior and development.* New York: Holt, Rinehart, & Winston, 1967.

Mead, G. *Mind, self, and society.* Chicago: University of Chicago Press, 1934.

Moustakas, C. (ed.). *Explorations in personal growth.* New York: Harper & Row, 1956.

Parsons, T., & K. Clark (eds.). *The Negro American.* Boston: Beacon Press, 1966.

Pettigrew, T. *A profile of the Negro American.* Princeton, N.J.: Van Nostrand, 1964.

Purkey, W. *Self-concept and school achievement.* Englewood Cliffs, N.J.: Prentice-Hall, 1970.

Rainwater, L. Crucible of identity: The Negro lower-class family. In T. Parsons & K. Clark (eds.), op. cit.

Rogers, C. *Client-centered therapy.* Boston: Houghton-Mifflin, 1951.

Snygg, D., & A. Combs. *Individual behavior.* Harper & Row, 1949.

Strong, D., & D. Feder. Measurement of the self-concept: A critique of the literature. *Journal of Counseling Psychology,* 1961, 8, 170.

Sullivan, H. *Conceptions of modern psychiatry.* Washington, D.C.: William Alanson White Foundations, 1947.

Wylie, R. *The self-concept: A critical survey of pertinent research literature.* Lincoln: University of Nebraska Press, 1961.

2

antecedent conditions of the development of self-concept in black americans

What color is Santa Claus? Some United States department stores are installing black Santas for their black customers. In Detroit's J. L. Hudson emporium, mother and children have their choice of lining up for eight white Santas or two black Santas. But 75 percent of the blacks have chosen the white Santas....

Time Magazine, December 14, 1970. Reprinted by permission
from TIME The Weekly Newsmagazine; Copyright Time Inc.

The Negro could not become indistinguishable from other Americans merely by changing his name, his speech, his style. Color was his continuing badge of inferiority.

Kenneth B. Clark, *Argument: The Complete Oral Argument*
Before The Supreme Court in Brown vs. Board of Education of Topeka,
1952-1955, p. xliv

...We're reared in houses with flies and roaches, with roofs that leak when it rains, with rickety old furniture that's fallin' apart, without even a coat of paint on the outside. Bein' black is in the air you breathe, and from the time you are a baby, your momma and daddy tell you how the white folks hate you and how you gotta be careful how you deal with 'em or they can kill you jus' as quick as they'd step on a bug. And you see that hostility all round you. Sometimes it's open and raw, other times it's subtle, but it's always there, it dogs your heels like a shadow. When you're black, most times your childhood jus' ain't no fun at all....

Excerpt from PLAYBOY Interview
with Charles Evers. Originally appeared in PLAYBOY
Magazine; copyright © 1971 by Playboy.

Brown vs. Board of Education and the
Black Self-Concept

A study of the self-concepts of young black children in Kansas served as a prominent basis in the argument for the plaintiffs during the landmark desegregation case *Brown* vs. *Board of Education, Topeka, Kansas,* 1952-55.*The lawyer for Brown et al. cited a study conducted by Dr. Kenneth B. Clark in which he presented sixteen white dolls and sixteen black dolls to sixteen pupils in an all black elementary school in Topeka. These pupils ranged in age from six to nine years. The pupils were asked to select the doll they would prefer, the doll they thought was nice, the doll that looked bad, and the doll that looked most like themselves. Ten out of the sixteen children preferred the white doll. Seven of these children thought the white doll looked most like themselves and nine of the children thought the white doll, as opposed to the black doll, was nice. Eleven of the children said that the black doll was bad but only one child said the white doll was bad (Friedman, 1969).

*For a detailed analysis of the admission of social science data into the court record, see *Argument,* L. Friedman (ed.), New York: Chelsea House Publishers, 1969.

While this study was used by Brown's attorney as evidence of the harmful effects of segregated schools, the attorney for the Board of Education introduced a similar study also conducted by Clark and Clark (1947) in nonsegregated schools in the North and South. In this study the Clarks used 253 black children aged two to seven years. They found that 62 percent of the black children in the South chose a white doll; 72 percent in the North chose the white doll; 52 percent of the children in the South thought the white doll looked nice; 68 percent of the children in the North thought the white doll looked nice. Forty-nine percent of the children in the South thought the black doll looked bad; 71 percent of the children in the North thought the black doll looked bad.

Although Professor Clark's studies are of interest to most people because of their bearing on the final decision of the court in favor of Brown et al., and because they served as a major breakthrough in the admission of social science data as legal evidence in a court of law, they are of interest in the context of the present discussion because they serve to point out the very early age (some children in the study were only two years old) at which black children had begun to evidence some form of a negative self-image. These black children had, in some manner, come to see white as nice and to be preferred, while black was bad. Professor Clark concluded that segregation in the schools served to harm the development of the children's concepts of themselves. However, after reviewing the results of the study of those black children who had attended nonsegregated schools in the North, we must conclude that variables other than, or in addition to, school segregation were operating to influence the negative view of self held by these children. In this chapter we will discuss empirically and theoretically some of these variables and the processes by which they come to impinge on the developing self-concepts of black Americans.

However, let us first reemphasize that the empirical research which has been done in this area has been unsystematic and inconclusive at best. One of the most difficult problems facing the researcher attempting to study self-concepts held by a minority group, especially American blacks, is separating the effects of ethnicity from the effects of socioeconomic status. The majority of empirical research on black Americans has been carried out on poor, rural Southern blacks or on slum dwelling urban Northern blacks. The results of these studies have then been generalized to all black Americans across geographical and social-class lines. It has been posited (Deutsch & Brown, 1964) that as the social-class level increases the cumulative deficit of being barred from "participation in the cultural mainstream" causes the impact of membership in a minority race to become even more intense and crucial. It may mean that being black is proportionately more detrimental to the upper and middle class American than it is to persons in the lower class.

Argyle (1968) has suggested that the three major influences on the development of self-concept are: (1) communication directly from other people about the self; (2) comparison of the self with others in the immediate environment; and (3) the role assigned to the self by his community. The first two of Argyle's sources of self are not unlike Cooley's (1902) notion of the "looking glass self."

Influences of the Home and Family Structure on the Black Self

The home and family life of an individual play a major role as the source of each of Argyle's bases for establishing a self-image. In the home, the individual frequently receives direct communication from other family members about his self. Further, he consistently uses these family members as yardsticks to measure his development of self, and finally, the position of the home, both geographically and socially, in the community determines in part the role assigned to the self by the family members. In fact, the black lower-class home has been described as the "crucible of identity" (Rainwater, 1966), suggesting perhaps that the individual's identity is, figuratively speaking, tested out or molded within the environs of the home.

Matriarchal Family Structure and Father Absence

If the family plays such a crucial role in providing the antecedent conditions which give rise to the developing self, the family life of lower-class black Americans should be carefully examined. Until recently, the most striking single aspect of lower-class black family life cited by investigators has been the predominantly **matriarchal** structure of power and influence. Rainwater, extrapolating from 1960 United States Census data, suggests that it is entirely possible that "as many as two-thirds of Negro urban poor children will not live in families headed by a man and woman throughout the first eighteen years of their lives" (Rainwater, 1966).

However, an increasing number of investigators are beginning to question the assertion that black families are more **matriarchal** than white families. Baughman (1971) questions "the validity of the proposition that intact black families are *markedly* (italics his) more **matriarchal** than intact white families." Hyman and Reed (1969) suggest that this is a question still in need of further empirical investigation rather than a truth to be accepted without critical analysis. A most interesting study in this area was reported by Bridgette (1970) who found that both black and white children tended to be more involved with their mothers, rather than fathers, in their day-to-day existence. However, proportionately more children of both races reported the father rather than the mother was the boss at home. While more white children than black children reported their fathers were bosses, there was no statistically significant difference between the children of the two races.

The **matriarchal** black family structure, if it exists, probably results from a combination of father absence, residual effects of plantation era life styles, unequal employment opportunities, and the functional autonomy available to many black women in an urban setting. It is interesting to note that in rural settings there is a very low proportion of mother-dominated families among lower-class blacks. Apparently vocational and economic demands require that the man serve a useful purpose in the rural black household and that he function to sustain the nuclear family in this setting.

Effects of Father Absence on the Young Child

The effects of mother-dominated, father-absent homes on the development of self-image in young children have been discussed by a number of writers (Frazier, 1962; Drake & Cayton, 1962; Pettigrew, 1964a, 1964b; Erikson, 1966; Rainwater, 1966; Proshansky & Newton, 1968).

Erikson believes that black mothers are likely to cultivate the "surrendered identity" which has been demanded of black males for generations. He suggests that the positive identity of the black American male has been eroded by the consistently "negative" reflections mirrored to him by the institutions of slavery in North America and the current constraints placed on him in the rural South and the urban North.

Some indirect evidence of the effects of matriarchal family life was reported in a study of the drawings of human figures of young "culturally deprived" black children living in a Northern urban area. It was found that *both* boys and girls coming from poor black families drew a greater number of more complete women than men (Dodd & Randall, 1966). This finding seems especially relevant to the development of an appropriate sex identity for the black male. The acquisition of an appropriate sex identity for the young black male is often made increasingly difficult because of the absence of a father or a father figure in the home who can serve as a model for sex-appropriate behavior.

Some data indicate that the rate of father absence in black families is as high as 50 percent in some regions, as compared to the national norm of approximately 10 percent (Moynihan, 1965; Pettigrew, 1964a).

There is also evidence that lower-class black males from father-absent homes are rated by teachers as being significantly more maladjusted than lower-class black males from father-present homes (Cortes & Fleming, 1968). The father-absent boys were seen by their teachers as being socially immature, consistently depressed and unhappy, more emotionally insecure, impulsive, moody, and inclined to be angry and irritable. In addition, the father-absent boys preferred male teachers to female teachers at a statistically significant level. There is some indication (Hetherington, 1966) that the most crucial period for a father to be present is during the first four years of the child's life.

Research on father-absent homes generally indicates that the key mediators in determining the quality of the psychological adjustment of the child are (1) recall of the father; (2) presence of another appropriate male figure; (3) the emotional stability of the mother; and (4) the socioeconomic status of the family. Optimum psychological adjustment appears to occur when the child has pleasant and fond memories of the absent father; where there are one or more appropriate male figures (relative or family friends) available for observation and interaction; where the mother remains emotionally stable and mediates the absence of the father in a positive and supportive manner, and when the family is at the middle- or upper-class level, socioeconomically.

Conversely, the conditions most detrimental to the development of a positive identity occur when the memories of the absent father are unpleasant or produce tension and anxiety in the child; when there are no male figures available to the child or when the available male figures provide inappropriate role models for the child; when the mother is emotionally unstable and consistently presents a negative picture of the absent father to the child; and when the family is in a lower socioeconomic position. In many instances the circumstances surrounding a father-absent black family tend to meet most of the conditions previously described as detrimental to a positive self-image, especially for the young male. Lacking an appropriate male model in the home, either real or mediated by other family members, the young black male adopts the available (although inappropriate from society's framework) behavioral role he observes or begins to look elsewhere outside the immediate or extended family for a role model. There is some evidence (Kardiner & Ovesey, 1962) to indicate that in the majority of lower-class black families the fathers, even when present, are somewhat passive and ineffective in family interactions. It has been suggested that the presence of such a weak, dependent, ineffectual male model may actually cause more harm than the absence of a positive male model (Herzog & Sudia, 1968).

Boys who were separated from their fathers before the age of five years have been found to be less masculine, more highly dependent on peers, less assertive, and engaged in fewer physical contact activities than boys from father-present homes (Hetherington, 1966). Research suggests that white father-present boys are the most masculine boys in terms of projective sex role orientation as measured by Brown's *IT Scale*. There appeared to be no significant difference between white father-absent boys and black father-present boys, while black father-absent boys were the least masculine of the four groups. It has also been found that white boys have a significantly higher masculinity score than do black boys. Additionally, father-present boys seems to have a significantly higher masculinity score than father-absent boys (Biller, 1968). It would appear that a boy who is reared in an environment which does not provide opportunities for him to interact with and imitate powerful and competent males is severely limited in developing a masculine sex-role orientation. As has been previously suggested by Kardiner and Ovesey (1962), the high incidence of matriarchical, passive-father homes found in lower-class black families frequently fails to provide appropriate sex role orientation opportunities for young males.

Other evidence suggests that father-absent four- and five-year-old black males are less aggressive, more dependent on adults and less masculine than father-present boys; however, boys from father-absent homes who have older brothers are more masculine than those father-absent boys who have older sisters. Father-absent girls are generally found to be more aggressive and less dependent if they have older male siblings (Santrock, 1970). Although the data suggest that older siblings can attenuate the negative effects of father absence on the development of self-image in young males and females, other data indicate that the presence of a father is more important in the development of masculinity in kindergarten-age boys than are male siblings (Biller, 1968).

Effects of Father Absence on Adolescents

When adolescent-aged subjects were studied, the results were somewhat contradictory to Biller's findings among young preschool children. Nobers (1968) found that black mothers in father-absent families display both instrumental (masculine) and expressive (feminine) roles and that their sons learned both roles. The white mothers in father-absent families studied by Nobers presented only an expressive role and their sons learned only this feminine role. He found that the father-absent white sons are significantly more feminine-expressive than black or white father-present sons and are significantly more feminine in identification than the father-absent black adolescents.

The seeming contradiction between the studies of Biller and the study of Nobers may possibly be explained on the basis of the age of the subjects studied. It may well be that the presence of a father in a black family during the preschool years is much more crucial than at the later adolescent stage in the development of sex role identification. Father absence, while harmful to the white child during the first four or five years of his life, may not be as crucial since he may have a wider availability of contact with adult males who can serve as appropriate models. Older black adolescents who have increased their range of contacts with adults outside of the home may be able to find appropriate male adult models at school, at YMCAs, in Big Brother-type organizations and other agencies. An increasing number of black professional athletes are going into lower-class black neighborhoods to work with young males and either directly or indirectly provide masculine role models for some young blacks.

It is interesting to note, however, that many young, lower-class black males who have a rather unmasculine underlying sex-role orientation frequently act very masculine in terms of their overt behavior. This tendency has been reported by at least two researchers working independently (Barclay & Cusumano, 1967; Biller & Borstelman, 1967). It was suggested that such overt masculine behavior may be a form of compensatory reaction against sex-role conflict which causes the boy to deny anything associated with femininity. Boys who are unmasculine in their sex-role orientation may also have to learn to overtly appear masculine in order to gain the approval of their peer group. In fact, Miller (1958) has postulated that the toughness and highly masculine-oriented peer group interaction found among lower-class gangs formed by male adolescents may result from the disproportionately higher number of fatherless homes found at this socioeconomic level. He suggests these adolescents may be attempting to compensate for the essentially feminine orientation of their home life. This observation may be especially valid for the lower-class black male reared in a matriarchical setting.

Data suggest that the father can be an important reinforcing agent for the development of appropriate sex role behavior in his daughter (Biller & Weiss, 1970). It may be that from a constructive interplay between father and daughter comes an opportunity for the daughter to learn specific aspects of the feminine role which will help to shape her identity. However, one research study (Santrock, 1970) found no differences in preschool black girls on dependency, aggression or femininity as a function of father absence.

Hetherington and Deur (1971) in a well-written article, stress that studies of father-absent girls indicate a reverse pattern when compared with studies of father-absent boys in regard to the time of onset of deviant behavior. Whereas the deviant behavior of father-absent boys is often evident at preschool ages, the deviant behavior of father-absent females emerges rather gradually and becomes clear only by the time of puberty. In contrast to father-absent males who have difficulty in acquiring a masculine sex role orientation, father-absent girls more commonly demonstrate inappropriate behavior patterns in relating to males rather than inappropriate feminine sex typing. Based on their own research (Hetherington & Deur, 1970), they feel that father-absent girls demonstrate two general types of disruption in heterosexual behavior. These girls tend to demonstrate severe sexual anxiety, shyness, and discomfort around males, or they tend to act in a promiscuous and inappropriately assertive manner when they are in the company of male figures. The former syndrome was most frequently found when the father's absence was a result of death. It may not be implausible to suggest that a number of girls first submit to heterosexual intercourse as a means of pleasing male friends, because they are certain that this type of interaction will establish or sustain a relationship which they do not know how to handle in any other manner. There is substantial evidence to indicate that female delinquents (a large majority of whom come from father- or mother-absent homes) are most frequently arrested for sexual violations (Cohen, 1955; Glaser, 1965).

Hetherington and Deur (1971) caution that care must be taken in interpreting studies of the effects of father absence. They contend that some of the findings regarding social and psychological maladjustment found in father-absent homes may reflect stress or conflict conditions occurring in the home rather than the effects of father absence per se. A number of studies are cited by Hetherington and Deur to support their contention. The studies reported suggest that many of the ill effects of broken homes result from the general instability of the home life rather than solely from paternal-absence. At least one study (Nye, 1957) concludes that an unhappy intact home may provide a more detrimental environment for the psychological development of the child than a home broken by divorce.

Effects of Husband-Father Absence on Mothers

Finally, the effects of husband-father absence on the mothers who remain in the homes should be considered.

The matriarchal power structure present in many lower-class black homes was discussed in an earlier portion of this chapter. There is some indication (Parker & Kleiner, 1965) that mothers in father-absent homes evidence more symptoms of psychiatric disorders than do black mothers living in an intact home. It is uncertain whether the father absence caused the presence of these psychiatric disorders or whether the pathological symptoms caused the father to flee the home. Regardless of cause and effect, it remains that children who are reared in these homes will be placed in a less healthy psychological milieu than children reared in more "normal" intact homes. It has been further suggested that the mother in a husband-father absent home may become hostile toward males, experience some guilt feelings about her adequacy as a wife, and feel strong financial pressure as a result of the absence of a male bread winner (Lerner, 1954). It is not unlikely that these mothers consciously or unconsciously mediate their negative perceptions to the children and that many of these perceptions become internalized by the young child in his/her developing notion of self and the world.

Essentially, the research data in the area of the effects of father absence are asserting that consideration must be given to the reason for the father's absence in order to interpret more validly the possible effects that this absence will have on the psychological development of the children. For instance, father absences caused by the death of the father may precipitate different outcomes among the mother and children than father absences caused by divorce, separation, or desertion. It is argued that absence caused by divorce, desertion, or separation is most frequently preceded by some considerable family conflict and, thus, is more likely to have a negative effect on the mother and the subsequent development of the children. If this is true, and it would seem to have a logical validity, it appears to carry major implications for lower-class black families where, all too frequently, separation, divorce, and desertion serve to produce father-absent families with the familial tension that so often accompanies this situation. In many lower-class black families an additional factor is frequently introduced into the father-absent homes. This factor is the new male figure or figures who frequently come to call on the mother following the father's absence. These suitors are sometimes presented to young children as "uncles" or "cousins" who have come to call or, in some instances, to live with the family for a time. Rainwater (1966) describes two types of boyfriends frequently found in these homes. One type is the boyfriend who "pimps" off the mother by demanding food or money from the woman in exchange for the privilege of his company. This arrangement has given rise, according to Rainwater, to what is called "Mother's Day," the tenth of each month when the AFDC checks arrive and the parties begin. The second type of boyfriend described by Rainwater may be more numerous than the pimp. This boyfriend, rather than getting paid for his services, actually contributes to the family's income in order to buy his way into a type of pseudo-family membership. Although this male does not assume the direct authority role of the father, he is frequently respected and liked by the children. Often, at least one of the children may actually have been fathered by this boyfriend. These boyfriends may drift from one girlfriend's house to another as time passes since no marital-like commitments are made between the man and woman. Rainwater reports that this less complex arrangement seems mutually accepted by both parties, since they can have the good parts of a man-woman relationship without having to endure the complexities that a marriage might produce.

These, then, are the types of environments in which many young lower-class blacks learn their sex roles. The family structure is frequently **matriarchal** in nature apparently because of father absence. The male figures in this milieu often emphasize expressive, affectional methods of getting by in their society. These male models work the angles of the system and learn to beat the Establishment at its own game. They are economically emasculated and are forced to adopt braggadocio social roles to compensate for this emasculation. The black female role models demonstrate to the young girls an extreme need to avoid becoming dependent on a man for anything that is essential to their well being. These models emphasize that a black woman in their world must become autonomous in terms of managing her own affairs and must learn to dominate the men in her immediate life space.

It is not our contention that this is the normative milieu for all or even most black families. However, it does occur with sufficient frequency that the adult who may be interacting with lower-class blacks should be sensitive to the possibilities of its existence and the influence it exerts on the developing self of the young black.

The Extended Family

Another major characteristic of lower-class black homes is the large number of relatives living in the same house. Frequently, as many as three generations are living under the same roof along with assorted uncles, aunts, cousins, and adopted kin. The extended family structure is more common both among lower- and middle-class blacks than among whites. The addition of relatives outside the mother-father-children triad often results in the grandmother becoming the head of the house if no husband-father is present. It is commonly found, however, that the majority of young black couples who marry set up their own households, and it is only after these marriages are dissolved that the mother will drift back to her parents and/or grandparents with any children produced during the marriage (Rainwater, 1966, p. 169).

The young child who is reared in a grandmother-dominated, extended family household may have some difficulty in finding available role models to utilize in developing an appropriate self-image. The mother, who should be the logical adult model, is all too often seen by her children as a person who is as weak as they are since she, too, is dominated by the grandmatriarch of the family.

Family Size

Added to the problems brought about by the extended family is the fact that lower-class black families generally have more children than do lower-class white families or middle-class black families (Rainwater, 1966, p.

170). Baughman and Dahlstrom (1968) report that 59 percent of black mothers said they were not pleased to learn that they were pregnant whereas only 23 percent of white mothers said they were not pleased to learn of their pregnant condition. This may suggest that more black than white children begin their life in an environment in which they are not wanted by their mothers. The presence of more people adds to the complexities of the mother and grandmother role if only in terms of physically providing and caring for their needs. Any psychological support and nurturance received by children in this type of family structure may be fleeting and haphazard at best. In this setting, mental health should probably best be defined in terms of survival.

Child-Rearing Practices

Lower-class black homes are often characterized by rather laissez-faire attitudes toward the care of the young compared with the deep psychological commitment usually found in both middle-class black and white homes. Frequently, small children are left to be cared for by aged grandparents who are too infirm and senile to be of much protection for the child, or they are left to be tended by siblings who are, themselves, barely competent for self-care. It is not uncommon for six-year-olds to be left as babysitters for their much younger siblings while mother goes to work for the day. Coopersmith (1967) has found three conditions in the home life which tend to generate feelings of worth and esteem among the children reared in these homes: (1) *parental warmth,* a feeling of love and concern for the child and a deep commitment to the child as a person on the part of the parents; (2) *respectful treatment,* familial interaction system in which the child's views are accorded attention and respect due any member of a democratic institution; and (3) *clearly defined limits,* a set of demands and expectations by the parents which clearly communicate to the child that they care for and are concerned about his well being. Although Coopersmith's research was done with white, middle-class boys it would seem logical that when these three conditions are met in the home, children would tend to develop high self-esteem regardless of ethnic group or social class. However, Baughman (1971) cautions that we should be extremely careful in transferring data and findings from white to black populations. There are data which suggest that black lower-class mothers tend to interact with their children in a manner which limits communication of respect for the child (Bernstein 1960; 1961; Hess & Shipman, 1965). They tend to use a status-oriented communication and control system when interacting with their children in teaching-learning situations and in disciplining their children. Status orientation is demonstrated by a mother watching television who tells her young child to be quiet and to quit banging the pots and pans he is using as toys. No attempt is made by this mother to explain to the child the causal connection between his banging activities and the mother's inability to hear the television set. The child is simply told to be quiet because "*I* (the mother in the higher status role) said so."

Black middle-class mothers, however, tend to use a more person-oriented elaborative mode of interacting with their children. In this case, the mother might explain to the young child that his pot and pan banging makes it very hard for her to hear what is being said on the television and if he wishes to bang on the pans he should go into the other room where his noise making will not interrupt the activities of other people. It is made clear that the child's rights are important to the mother, but that it is necessary for the child to consider the rights of others at the same time. The child learns that he must leave the room not simply because his mother said so and because she has more rank in the home than he, but because his activities are interfering with another person's rights. It is not suggested that middle-class mothers *never* resort to a status oriented mode of interaction with their children or that lower-class mothers *never* use a person-oriented approach, but that there is a greater tendency for middle-class black mothers to use the person-oriented approach more consistently and for lower-class black mothers to use the status-oriented approach more consistently.

Agencies Outside the Home: Community Life Styles

Although the home serves as a crucial arena in which developing concepts of self are played out by various family members, there are also many opportunities for the black child to obtain information which shapes his notion of self outside the home. Within the lower-class black society, Rainwater (1966) describes three types of survival strategies employed by the inhabitants. The first of these strategies is the *expressive life style*. This mode of living involves making oneself as attractive and interesting as possible to other people in order to control them in a manipulative fashion, so that immediate needs are satisfied. Many lower-class blacks become quite adept at this persuasion process and develop smooth lines of patter which charm and disarm acquaintances and strangers alike. This manipulation of people through personal charisma and verbal facility is sometimes called "working game" by the street inhabitants who practice it. Rainwater suggests that when the *expressive style* does not work or is unavailable for one reason or another, the lower-class black is tempted to resort to another survival strategy—the *violent strategy*. This strategy dictates that if the person cannot use verbal or charismatic attributes to gain his objective, then force must be used. The third strategy, the *depressive strategy*, is adopted increasingly as lower-class blacks grow older. In this strategy, the goals of life are constantly lowered until they consist merely of obtaining those things necessary to keep the body, but not necessarily the spirit, alive. This strategy is best described as an "I won't bother you if you won't bother me" outlook on life.

Rainwater (1966) and Miller (1958) have suggested that the majority of lower-class people go through life alternating in a cyclic fashion from one strategy to another. They go from the peak of the expressive strategy through the desperation of the violent strategy to the hopelessness of the depressive strategy. It is within this frame of reference that the young black child begins to develop his notions of self and of his place in the world. His self-image is reflected back to him intermittently by exhilarated mirrors, by desperate mirrors, and by dissolute mirrors.

Charles Evers (1971) tells of returning home from a church service where the preacher had told the rural black congregation that "All God's children are the same and nobody's different from anybody else." Evers asked his father, "Why are *we* different? The preacher don't say we gotta be different." His father, who had seemingly already adopted Rainwater's depressed strategy, replied, "Well, son, that's the way it is, and they ain't nothin' we can do about it. 'Cause if we try to do anything about it, they kill us." Evers later says that as strong a man as his father was, he had given up hope of ever changing the system.

The community in which the black individual is reared is frequently in a segregated black neighborhood where the members of the community often label each other as "black boy," "black-assed," "black-bastard" and other black-oriented appellations. The child is repeatedly exposed to the idea that blacks perceive black as being bad or as denoting negative traits. The child may develop negative perceptions of self and other blacks as a result of this exposure within his community. In a number of ways the neighborhood serves as a source for each of the three major influences on self-concept suggested by Argyle (1968) earlier in the chapter. The neighborhood determines those people who will provide direct communication to a person about himself; it determines those people with whom the individual will compare himself; and, it determines the role assigned to the individual by his community. Rainwater (1966) says,

> In this way, one of the effects of ghettoization is to mask the ultimate enemy so that the understanding of the fact of victimization by a caste system comes as a late acquisition laid over conceptions of self and of other Negroes derived from intimate, and to the child often traumatic, experience within the ghetto community.

Purkey (1970) succinctly summarizes the impact of the neighborhood on the developing self by quoting a portion of W. Somerset Maugham's *The Razor's Edge:*

For men and women are not only themselves; they are also the region in which they were born, the city apartment or the farm in which they learned to walk, the games they played as children, the old wives' tale they overheard, the food they ate, the schools they attended, the sports they followed, the poems they read, and the God they believed in.

Schools

If a black child attends a ghetto school where his black teachers confirm, either consciously or by inference, the negative conceptions of blackness supported by his ghetto community, the child is likely to have a difficult time developing a realistic image of himself. The self of a black person, like the self of a white person, cannot develop or exist in and of itself. The self must always develop and exist vis-à-vis the family, vis-à-vis the peer group, and vis-à-vis the community and world at large.

Research by psychologists and sociologists has identified other factors that might serve as antecedent conditions influencing the emergence of the black self. These factors are racial identity, geographic residence, and skin color.

Racial Identity and Geographic Residence

A number of studies have supported the general finding that black children are aware of their racial identity at a rather early age. Horowitz (1939) and Stevenson and Stewart (1958) report that racial awareness and distinction definitely increase with age and that a sharp increase in awareness occurs between three and four years of age. They further report that racial preference is well defined by the age of seven. Raymer (1969) has found that racial identification occurs as early as age three among some children. She reports that four-year-old black and white children from a lower-socioeconomic status population preferred the white race over the black race as evidenced from their responses to a 96-item paired-picture selection task. The presence of a black examiner did not seem to alter the children's preference for the white race.

Morland (1966) has studied the perceptions of young black and white nursery school children in the mid-South by using a picture choice technique in a different manner than that used in Raymer's study. His subjects lived in highly segregated neighborhoods and Morland was attempting to determine how they viewed themselves as individuals (self-image) and how they identified themselves in racial terms. He found that the majority of the children of both races perceived themselves as being "white." The majority of children from both races said they would rather be "white," and that the white woman (in the picture) looked most like their mother. Morland (1968) later expanded the original purposes of his investigations into race awareness among children to include a comparison of the development of this trait in Southern children and Northern children. The Southern subjects were located in Lynchburg, Virginia and lived in tightly segregated conditions while the Northern subjects lived in Boston, Massachusetts in much less segregated conditions. Morland was able to match his subjects on age and sex, and although he could not precisely control the factors of intelligence and socioeconomic level, he reports that the distribution was fairly equal. Pictures of young white and black children and white and black adults were used as stimuli. In this particular study, Morland was interested in studying racial acceptance, racial preference, racial self-identification and racial identification ability. He found that almost all of the children of both races accepted whites, only Southern whites rejected children because of race. In terms of racial preference, he found that all the groups preferred whites while the Southern blacks were least likely and Southern whites most likely to prefer their own race. Generally, however, the majority of the children in all four groups (Northern whites, Northern blacks, Southern blacks, and Southern whites) tended to accept the other race. On measures of racial self-identification, the white children were more likely to say they looked like the white children in the pictures than black children were to say they looked like the black children in the picture. The majority of white children "would rather be white," while only one half of the black children "would rather be black." The whites were also more likely to identify their mothers as members of their own race than the blacks were. The last trait studied by Morland, racial recognition ability, involved the subjects' ability to "find a white person in this picture" or "do you see a black person in this picture." Findings indicated that the Southern whites were significantly better at identifying the different races than any of the other three groups.

Morland concluded that, in general, the findings of his previous study on Southern blacks and whites tended to hold up along regional lines; that is, whites tend to identify with and prefer members of their own race while blacks tend to prefer and identify with members of the opposite race. There are some minor regional differences in this respect since the differences between white and black tend to be accentuated in the Southern sample. These differences are interpreted by Morland to be related to the greater emphasis on being white in the Southern segregated society. He suggests that the realization of their correct racial membership and their actual position in society can be a traumatic experience for Southern blacks. Although Morland's sample of subjects was not truly randomized and some question therefore remains as to its representativeness of the population he was attempting to study, his findings are not inconsistent with the results of Raymer's study cited previously, the studies by Clark and Clark presented in the opening sections of this chapter, and the results of the Stevenson and Stewart study (1958).

Development of Color Awareness in Children

Some general conclusions which are suggested by the studies in the area of racial identity and awareness are that the ability to discriminate physical differences between blacks and whites develops rapidly during the preschool years. Generally, whites (especially Southern whites) develop this discriminatory ability more rapidly than any other group. One explanation which has been advanced for the relatively lower discriminatory ability among blacks is that black children live in a "white world" while whites who live in segregated neighborhoods and attend segregated schools do not experience the "black world." Since it may be hypothesized that children will perceive objects as being different to the degree that the characteristics deviate from those encountered in their daily lives, it can be predicted that white children might perceive the physical characteristics of blacks as being relevant bases for selecting individuals as being different more than young black children living in a "white dominated world" would perceive the familiar characteristics of whites as being distinctive and relevant (Stevenson & Stewart, 1958).

The general findings of these studies suggest once more that young black children have more negative attitudes toward themselves and their race and would prefer the white race. The most frequent explanation for this attitude proposed by psychologists, psychiatrists, and sociologists is that the black child lives in a white-oriented world where white is consistently presented as the good and desirable trait while black is mediated as the trait to be avoided and demeaned. This explanation is vividly illustrated by a statement of Charles Evers (1971) concerning growing up black in the South.

> So many parents would up and tell their kids, 'It's a white man's world and you jus' happen to be here, nigger.' And black kids saw all the power and all the money and all the decent livin' on the side of the whites, and a lot of 'em thought, hell, there must be somethin' wrong with us to live like this. I mean, even the standards of beauty you'd see in papers and magazines and movies were all white standards; black kids grew up thinkin' they was *ugly*, and nothin' destroys self-respect more than that.

It is too early to determine what effects such national movements as black-power advocacy, black-studies programs, "black is beautiful" campaigns, black economic progress on many fronts, integrated schools and neighborhoods, and nondiscriminatory hiring and firing practices will have on the developing perceptions of self held by young blacks in the coming years. There is some evidence to indicate that no matter how economically and socially successful the black individual becomes, he still must face many problems that accrue to him merely because he is a black person living in a white-oriented world. As one unidentified race and education conference participant reported (Kvaraceus, et al., 1965) "...You can't grow up a Negro, even a middle-class Negro, without knowing many defeats and discriminations just because of who you are." Further examples can be given of "successful" black movie stars, scholars, writers, athletes, and business executives who cannot escape the stigma of being born black no matter how well they develop the skills and competencies of their profession and no matter how great a contribution they make to society as individual citizens. A large measure of this stigma may be related to the mere fact that these people, like their racial brothers, have, in varying degrees, the stereotypical phenotype of the black person.

Skin Color

One of the most salient phenotypic characteristics which characterizes the black person is his skin color. No amount of changes in economic or social status can alter the fact that his skin is black. There is evidence that more and more blacks are coming to accept their skin color today as opposed to ten or twenty years ago (Ogletree, 1969), and that, among some blacks themselves, black skin may serve as an asset as opposed to a liability. Witness, for example, a recent statement made by a black writer: "It is interesting to note that all the major leaders among Negroes today tend to be quite Negroid in appearance. In fact, my black skin has a great value among Negroes today. I do remember a time when being as black as I am did not have much value, but today it is different" (Kvaraceus et al., 1965). Other studies, however, indicate that coming to grips with skin color is one of the most important aspects of the development of self faced by the black person.

A most unique and creative study carried out by Palmer and Masling (1969) presents information concerning the difficulty that black children and adolescents have in incorporating blackness into their self-images. Palmer and Masling suggested that an analysis of the language content of young blacks, particularly in regard to themes involving color, would provide some indication of their effort to come to terms with their skin color. They predicted that black children and adolescents would be more preoccupied with and would talk more about skin color than would white children and adolescents. To test this hypothesis they asked forty-eight youngsters to describe sixteen bubble-gum pictures of white and black baseball players. The youngsters were also asked to describe a series of "neutral" blue paint samples. The hypothesis of Palmer and Masling was supported. Black children used a significantly higher proportion of their verbal descriptions to talk about the skin colors of the baseball players depicted in the pictures than did the white children. Since there was no significant difference between the white and black subjects' descriptions of the blue paint samples, the investigators concluded that the difference in preoccupation with skin color by black youth was not a preoccupation with color per se. In commenting on the study by Palmer and Masling, McCandless (1970) suggests that black youth need to dwell on skin color for important reasons which are related to the development of self-concept. He says they need to do this in order "to gain in self-understanding, to rationalize, to re-evaluate and to produce self-concept congruency among other things."

It has also been found (Bayton & Muldrow, 1968) that college-age black males who perceive themselves as being relatively light skinned compared to other members of their race seemed to be the most sensitive group of blacks. Research findings indicated that these light-skinned black males occupied some "psychologically marginal status" which may sensitize them to cues regarding skin color emanating from their peers. There is further evidence to suggest that light-skinned males tend to be uncomfortable *vis-a-vis* dark skinned blacks.

Williams (1966) presents some intriguing data that may have an indirect bearing on the black person's conceptualization of skin color. He indicates that evaluative connotations of color names applied to racial groups are one determinant of the favorability of attitudes toward racial groups.

He found that blacks generally agreed with whites on meanings of color names when they were presented in a nonracial context, but they responded to racial concepts in a notably different manner. For example, the term "black person" might be interpreted by the black man as black *person*, but to the white man it connoted *black* person. Williams recommends that it might be advantageous to reshape our language habits in order not to designate groups of persons by evaluatively connoted color names, but he also recognizes that some whites may be reluctant to give up the term white since it carries positive evaluative connotations.

Once again, we can only hypothesize concerning the changes in the evaluative connotations of the color code black as a result of recent movements in the area of black pride and black power. Some researchers (Proshansky & Newton, 1968) have suggested that the light-skinned black in America has been accorded special favors within the middle- and upper-class society since the plantation days. Other writers (Coles, 1965; Grambs, 1965; Kardiner & Ovesey, 1962) have noted that black parents place a high premium on light-skinned offspring and dark-skinned men often try to marry light-skinned women.

Theoretical Positions Regarding Antecedents of the Black Self

Pettigrew (1964b) suggests that attempts to understand the personal-social consequences of being a black person in a white environment cannot advance without the development of appropriate social-psychological theory. Such theory, according to Pettigrew, must take into account the following major factors,

> (1) historical, social, and cultural forces which vitally affect black Americans; (2) the untold damage done by these forces to the inner-most depths of the black individual's personality; (3) the specific dynamics of and conditions under which these forces act upon the individual black person (p. 12).

Although the present authors are in agreement with Pettigrew that a theory containing these three elements is highly desirable in advancing the understanding of the black self, we suggest that until such theory is developed, current theories of personality development can be used as a general framework within which to conceptualize the development of the black self.

Ausubel's Satellization Theory

One theory of personality which appears to offer valuable direction in interpreting the developing black self is proposed by David P. Ausubel (1954). Three assumptions underlie his theory: (1) all behavior is motivated; (2) behavior is motivated toward maintaining or enhancing self-esteem; and (3) self-esteem is a function of status. According to Ausubel, there are four major sources of status or status conferring agencies: (1) family, especially parents, (2) peers, (3) teachers, and (4) significant others in the individual's environment. These status conferring agencies can grant two types of status, *derived* status and *primary* status.

Derived status is not unlike the ascribed status or positional status discussed by some sociologists. It is given as a result of the individual's family status or the status of organizations in which he holds membership. It is not given for anything the individual has accomplished on his own but for the position in society held by the person. Memberships in fraternities and sororities provide individuals with derived status. Similarly, being a member of the Vanderbilt or Rockefeller family would lend the individual derived status. *Primary* status is accorded individuals for developing executive competencies. That is, primary status is given to individuals who have developed outstanding skills and abilities which they can perform independently of their social position or background. Ausubel suggests that true primary status must be conferred by a broad segment of society and not merely by a small group of individuals. For example, the status accorded to members of adolescent gangs or cliques by other members of the same group for such executive competencies as "playing the dozens" or working a "hustle" is said to be a pseudo-primary status or interim status. True primary status is not easily accessible to the majority of children and adolescents, black or white.

In tracing the development of self, Ausubel suggests that each individual is in a stage of ego aggrandizement (inflated sense of self-worth) during the first two or two and one-half years of life. This ego aggrandized stage is characterized by the individual's being volitionally omnipotent (his will is all powerful, his wishes get carried out) but executively incompetent (he is unable to satisfy his wishes by himself). The child learns that while he cannot do things for himself (executive incompetence) he can get them done by making his wishes or desires known to his parents and family (volitional omnipotence). Gradually the child develops the notion that he must be a very powerful person, because he is able to order these larger, more potent adult figures to meet his needs. This inflated sense of self-worth generally lasts until the child is approximately two years of age. At about this time a combination of factors such as toilet training, demand by parents for language development, and increased demands for consideration of other people's rights, serve to apply pressure on the child to give up his exaggerated sense of self-worth and undergo the "crisis of ego devaluation." Although the process of ego devaluation is a rather gradual one for most children, it does represent, according to Ausubel, the first major crisis in the development of self.

After pressure is applied to the child to relinquish his feelings of self-grandeur, he must look for other sources of status and self-esteem. Ausubel suggests that the majority of children tend to seek a type of derived status from their parents by a process called "satellization." *Satellization* is similar to the Freudian concept of identification in that the child tends to adopt the parents' belief systems, attitudes, mores, social customs, and behavioral patterns. In return, the child receives derived status as a result of being known as the child of parents who have status and respect in the community. Ausubel describes six types of satellization relationships between parents and children: (1) over-dominated satellizer, (2) under-dominated satellizer, (3) over-protected satellizer, (4) under-protected satellizer, (5) over-appreciated satellizer, and (6) under-appreciated satellizer. These categories represent extremes on three continua describing the relationship between the child and parents. These categories are not quantitatively exact but merely reflect relative positions from a mid-point on each of the child-family relationships involving appreciation, dominance, and protection. It is suggested that one of these six categories is a "best fit" in describing the satellization relationship between the parents and the child.

A type of satellization relationship with parents exists for most children until the time of adolescence. At this time, a second major crisis point in the developmental history of an individual is reached. This crisis involves the process of "desatellizing" (breaking away from the satellizing relationship formerly held with the parents) versus nondesatellizing (remaining in a satellization relationship with the parents and remaining psychologically dependent on parents). The large majority of adolescents follow the route of desatellization from parents and begin to look to other sources as a basis for developing new attitudes, mores, belief systems, and values. Generally, the adolescent's peer group serves as the source from which these new frames of reference are developed. Hence, Ausubel suggests that most adolescents enter into a type of resatellization around the peer group after they desatellize from their parents. The peer group serves not only as a source for developing new perspectives but also as a medium for checking out and evaluating existing views.

It must be remembered, however, that the peer group cannot grant true primary status but is limited to a type of interim or pseudo-primary status. Ausubel does suggest that a few adolescents are able to obtain a true form of primary status after desatellizing from their parents and these persons seek this primary status route rather than the interim status offered them by their peer group. Examples of adolescents who seek this primary status orientation may be child-adolescent actors and actresses, certain musical prodigies, and teen-aged Olympic athletes. Primary status is granted on a broad societal basis and is much less available to adolescents than the interim status afforded them by membership in their own peer groups.

A third route to obtaining status available to the adolescent who has given up much of his derived status from family as a result of having desatellized, is *achievement orientation*. This orientation involves a type of self-conferred status. The adolescent does his own thing for the sake of doing it to the best of his abilities. He awards himself satisfaction for a job well done and does not seek the plaudits of society in general or even the appreciation of a smaller peer group. Although a small proportion of adolescents have appeared to take this route in the past, it is the opinion of the present authors that an increasing number of young people have opted for this status orientation in recent years.

Implications of Satellization Theory for the Black Self

In his discussion of the developmental differences which may occur among black children and youth, Ausubel and Ausubel (1963) observed that

...the ego development of segregated Negro children in America manifests certain distinctive properties. Negro children live in a predominantly lower class subculture that is further characterized by a unique type of family structure, by specially circumscribed opportunities for acquiring status, by varying degrees of segregation from the dominant white majority, and, above all, by a fixed and apparently immutable denigration of their social value, standing, and dignity as human beings because of their skin color. Hence, it would be remarkable indeed if these factors did not result in significant developmental differences in self-esteem, in aspirations for achievement, in personality adjustment, and in character structure (p. 109).

Ausubel suggests that the differences in child rearing practices between middle-class parents and lower-class parents have great import for ego development of the black child who more often than not comes from a lower-class environment. Lower-class parents tend to relinquish strict control of the child's activities much earlier than do middle-class parents. This fact increases the possibility that the peer groups will gain a much stronger control over the socialization of the lower-class child. Young, lower-class black children tend to undergo much of the desatellization process which does not commonly occur in middle-class homes until late childhood and early adolescence. This pattern tends to force the lower-class black child to develop skills related to independence and self-care much earlier. He is frequently forced to take on adultlike responsibilities and to develop "precocious independence." It has been pointed out (Ausubel & Ausubel, 1963) that *precocious independence* from family and the exaggerated socializing influence of the peer group is common to both lower-class black and white families, but not to lower-class Puerto Rican or lower-class Mexican-American families. The Ausubels cite research which indicates that Puerto Rican and Mexican children enjoy a more closely knit family life, characterized by intimate contact between parents and children. They further suggest that in the Mexican families the roles of fathers and mothers are very distinctive, and the young Mexican child develops a more clearly delineated conception of masculine and feminine roles within the family group. This lessens the influence of the socialization effect of the peer group.

Given the social, economic, and educational situations extant in society, it would seem that ego development in the black self is influenced by a number of factors over which the black person has little or no control. First, the black self has little chance to gain the derived status that is the cornerstone of self-esteem for all young children. The child can satellize only with parents or other superior individuals in his environment who themselves frequently have an inferior status. Second, the black self rarely has available appropriate adult satellization models. Not infrequently, the powerful adults in this child's environment obtained their preeminence through such activities as stealing, drug pushing, pimping, and other extralegal hustles. It must be tempting for the impressionable young black to identify with these powerful and highly visible figures in his world.

Desatellization and Black Youth

In some ways, the tenuous satellization experiences which the black self has with family figures may be advantageous. The desatellization process is rarely as traumatic for this child as it might be for the frequently over-protected middle-class child. The young black child often develops certain executive competencies which are necessary in his world at a young age, and some of these survival strategies and skills serve the developing black self well. At the same time, this precocious independence from parents may cause the black adolescent to have a stronger need for monetary resources at an earlier age and may lead him to forego extended periods of formal schooling in order to meet these financial needs.

Since the black self has a shortened satellization relationship with parents who are unable to provide a source of derived status, it is necessary to seek primary sources of ego support. Under ordinary circumstances the most available sources of primary status for the school-aged child are academic success, athletic prowess, artistic talents, and social finesse. For the black self, and particularly for the young black boy, most of these sources of primary status are usually not available or are not perceived as realistic and desirable priorities for survival. The host of factors associated with ghetto life tends to push many black boys toward athletics as a source of primary status. Many blacks have been able to rise from the ghetto to stardom and have become famous personalities, both on and off the field, court, and arena. Some black athletes return to their neighborhoods in the off-season to work with young blacks in various recreational and sports-related programs. They provide powerful and successful adult models around whom black children and youth can satellize. Partly because it makes good copy for the press, the actual impact of these efforts is sometimes drawn out of proportion. The number of success stories of black athletes, while fairly large in absolute numbers, is extremely small in terms of the number of boys who are able to follow this route to primary status. For every Walt Frazier, Willie Mays, Gale Sayers, and Arthur Ashe, there are many Earl Manigaults who achieve local fame in athletics, but then fade into a life of self-despair and self-destruction.[*]

Perhaps the most common route toward status among black adolescents, just as among white adolescents, is the interim or "pseudo-primary" status of the peer group. In middle-class society the peer group takes the form of cliques, secret clubs, sororities, and fraternities; in the lower classes it is most frequently labeled as a gang. The types of executive competencies (abilities or special skills) which are deemed important by each gang or peer group determine what each individual member must do in order

---

[*]For a description of the life of Earl Manigault and other black playground athletes who have attempted to use athletic skill as a path to primary status, see *The City Game* by Pete Axthelm, New York: Harper's Magazine Press, 1970.

to achieve status and self-esteem. In some groups the members must demonstrate skill in stripping a car of its marketable components in as short a time as possible or shoplifting desirable items to share or sell. Other lower-class peer aggregates and groups require such extralegal behaviors as smoking pot or even shooting up heroin in order to achieve status within the group. The psychological power of the peer group to control behavior by awarding or withholding status from its members is often as influential on the individual as the physically addictive power of drugs. Of course, not all clubs and peer groups require extralegal behaviors on the part of their members in order to achieve status, but an alarming number of groups with which the black self has contact in the ghetto do operate on such a basis. It is frequently difficult for a teacher or social worker who is attempting to work with lower-class adolescents to understand that, compared to the peer group, the helping professional is usually operating with an empty bag. Many adolescents who, for whatever reason, have been cut off from parent and parent-surrogate sources of status tend to look toward peers almost exclusively for ego support. In fact, adolescents must often deliberately resign their opportunities for status with adults in authority positions in order to achieve peer status. Teachers who, with the best of intentions, bestow lavish praise on adolescents in the presence of their peers believe that praise will give encouragement for the individual to repeat desired behaviors. Such teachers would do well to reconsider the effect that their behavior may have on the adolescent in light of the source from which he or she is seeking status.

In this chapter we have presented the major antecedents of the black self and demonstrated a theoretical approach which is potentially useful for adults working with young blacks as a framework to guide their understanding of the development of self esteem among black children and youth. While using this framework as a guide, however, it is important to remember the individual uniqueness of all human beings and to be sensitive to these differences when interpreting the actions of an individual.

References

Argyle, F. The self-concept of Negro and white school beginners. Paper presented at The Annual Meeting of the American Educational Research Association, Chicago, 1968.

Ausubel, D., & P. Ausubel. Ego development among segregated Negro children. In A. Passow (ed.), *Education in depressed areas.* New York: Columbia University Press, 1963.

Ausubel, D. *Theory and problems of adolescent development.* New York: Grune & Stratton, 1954.

Axthelm, P. *The city game.* New York: Harper's Magazine Press, 1970.

Barclay, A., & D. Cusumano. Father-absence, cross-sex identity, and field dependent behavior in male adolescents. *Child Development,* 1967, 38, 243-50.

Baughman, E. E. *Black Americans.* New York: Academic Press, 1971.

Baughman, E. E. and W. G. Dahlstrom. *Negro and white children: A psychological study in the rural South.* New York: Academic Press, 1968.

Bayton, J., & T. Muldrow. Interaction variables in the perception of racial personality traits. *Journal of Experimental Research in Personality,* 1968, 3, 39-44.

Bernstein, B. Social structure, language, and learning. *Educational Research,* 1961, 3, 163-76.

Bernstein, B. Language and social class. *British Journal of Sociology,* 1960, 11, 271-76.

Biller, H. A note on father absence and masculine development in lower class Negro and white boys. *Child Development,* 1968, 39, 1003-6.

Biller, H., & L. Borstelmann. Masculine development: An integrative review. *Merrill-Palmer Quarterly,* 1967, 13, 253-94.

Biller, H., & J. Weiss. The father-daughter relationship and the personality development of the female. *Journal of Genetic Psychology.* 1970, 116, 78-93.

Bridgette, R. E. Self esteem in Negro and white Southern adolescents. Unpublished doctoral dissertation, University of North Carolina at Chapel Hill, 1970.

Clark, K. The social scientists, the Brown decision, and contemporary confusion. In L. Friedman (ed.), *Argument.* New York: Chelsea House, 1969.

Clark, K., & M. Clark. Racial identification and preference in Negro children. In T. Newcomb, & E. Hartley (eds.), *Readings in Social Psychology.* New York: Holt, 1947.

Cohen, A. *Delinquent boys: The culture of the gang.* Glencoe, Illinois: Free Press, 1955.

Coles, R. It's the same but it's different. In T. Parsons, & K. Clark (eds.), *The Negro American.* Boston: Houghton-Mifflin, 1966.

Cooley, C. *Human nature and the social order.* New York: Scribner's, 1902.

Coopersmith, S. *The antecedents of self-esteem.* San Francisco: Freeman, 1967.

Cortes, C., & E. Fleming. The effects of father absence on the adjustment of culturally disadvantaged boys. *Journal of Special Education,* 1968, 2, 413-20.

Deutsch, M., & B. Brown. Social influences in Negro-white intelligence differences. *Journal of Social Issues,* 1964, 20, 24-35.

Deutsch, M., I. Katz, & A. Jensen (eds.). *Social class, race, and psychological development.* New York: Holt, Rinehart, & Winston, 1968.

Dodd, J., & R. Randall. A comparison of Negro childrens' drawings of a man and a woman. *Journal of Negro Education,* 1966, 35, 287-92.

Drake, S., & H. Cayton. *Black metropolis: A study of Negro life in a Northern City,* (rev. ed.) New York: Harper & Row, 1962 (2 vols.).

Erikson, E. The concept of identity in race relations: Notes and queries. In T. Parsons and K. Clark (eds.), *The Negro American.*

Evers, C. Playboy interview: Charles Evers. *Playboy,* October, 1971.

Frazier, E. *Black bourgeoisie.* New York: Collier, 1962.

Friedman, L. (ed.). *Argument: The Complete Oral Argument Before The Supreme Court in Brown vs. Board of Education of Topeka, 1952-1955.* New York: Chelsea House, 1969.

Glaser, D. Social disorganization and delinquent subcultures. In H. Quay (ed.), *Juvenile delinquency.* New York: Van Nostrand, 1965.

Grambs, J. The self-concept: Basis for reeducation of Negro youth. In W. Kvaraceus, et al. (eds.), *Negro self-concept: Implications for school and citizenship.* New York: McGraw-Hill, 1965.

Herzog, E., & C. Sudia. Fatherless homes: A review of research. *Children,* 1968, 5, 179.

Hess, R., & V. Shipman. Early blocks to children's learning. *Children,* 1965, 12, 189-94.

Hetherington, M. Effects of paternal absence on sex typed behaviors in Negro and white preadolescent males. *Journal of Personality and Social Psychology,* 1966, 4, 87-91.

Hetherington, M., & J. Deur. The effects of father-absence on personality development of daughters. Unpublished manuscript, University of Wisconsin, 1970.

Hetherington, M., & J. Deur. The effects of father-absence on child development. *Young Children,* 1971, 26, 4, 233-44.

Horowitz, R. Racial aspects of self-identification in nursery school children. *Journal of Psychology,* 7, 1939, 91-99.

Hyman, H. H., & J. S. Reed. "Black matriarchy" reconsidered: Evidence from secondary analysis of sample surveys. *Public Opinion Quarterly* 1969, *33* (3) 346-54.

Kardiner, A., & L. Ovesey. *The mark of oppression: Explorations in the personality of the American Negro.* Cleveland: World, 1962. (Paperback.)

Kvaraceus, W., J. Gibson, F. Patterson, B. Seasholes, & J. Grambs. *Negro self-concept: Implications for school and citizenship.* New York: McGraw-Hill, 1965.

Lerner, S. The effects of desertion on family life. *Social Casework,* 1954, 35, 3-8.

McCandless, B. *Adolescents: Behavior and development.* Hinsdale, Ill.: Dryden Press, 1970.

Miller, W. Lower class culture as a generating milieu of gang delinquency. *Journal of Social Issues,* 1958, 14, 5-19.

Morland, J. Racial self-identification: A study of nursery school children. *American Catholic Sociological Review,* 1968, 24, 231-42.

Morland, J. A comparison of race awareness in Northern and Southern children. *American Journal of Orthopsychiatry,* 1966, 36, 22-31.

Moynihan, D. *The Negro family: The case for national action.* Washington, D.C.: U.S. Government Printing Office, 1965.

Newcomb, T., E. Hartley (eds.). *Readings in Social Psychology.* New York: Holt, 1947.

Nobers, D. The effects of father-absence and mothers' characteristics on the identification of adolescent white & Negro males. *Dissertation Abstracts,* 1968, 29, 1508-9.

Nye, F. Child adjustment in broken and in unhappy, unbroken homes. *Marriage and Family Living,* 1957, 19, 356-61.

Ogletree, E. Skin color preference of the Negro child. *Journal of Social Psychology,* 1969, 79, 143-44.

Palmer, R., & J. Masling. Vocabulary for skin color in Negro and white children. *Developmental Psychology,* 1969, 1, 396-401.

Parker, S., & R. Kleiner. *Mental illness in the urban Negro community.* New York: Free Press, 1965.

Parsons, T., & K. Clark (eds.). *The Negro American.* Boston: Houghton-Mifflin, 1966.

Passow, A. (ed.). *Education in depressed areas.* New York: Columbia University Press, 1963.

Pettigrew, T. *A profile of the Negro American.* Princeton, N.J.: Van Nostrand, 1964a.

Pettigrew, T. Negro American personality: Why isn't more known? *Journal of Social Issues,* 1964b, 10, 4-23.

Proshansky, H., & P. Newton. The nature and meaning of Negro self-identity. In M. Deutsch, I. Katz, & A. Jensen (eds.), *Social class, race, and psychological development.* New York: Holt, Rinehart & Winston, 1968.

Purkey, W. *Self-concept and school achievement.* Englewood Cliffs, N.J.: Prentice-Hall, 1970.

Quay, H. (ed.). *Juvenile delinquency.* New York: Van Nostrand, 1965.

Rainwater, L. Crucible of identity: The Negro lower-class family. In T. Parsons and K. Clark (eds.), *Negro American.*

Raymer, E. Race and sex identification in preschool children. UCLA Center for Headstart Evaluation and Research, August, 1969. ERIC: ED 041 634.

Santrock, J. Paternal absence, sex typing, and identification. *Developmental Psychology,* 1970, 2, 264-72.

Stevenson, H., & E. Stewart. A developmental study of racial awareness in young children. *Child Development,* 1958, 29, 399-409.

Williams, J. Connotations of racial concepts and color names. *Journal of Personality and Social Psychology,* 1966, 3, 531-40.

3

personal control and the black self

The whole act's immutably decreed: 'Twas rehearsed by thee and me a billion years before this ocean rolled. Fool! I am the Fate's lieutenant. I act under orders.

Ahab in H. Melville, *Moby Dick*

Men at some time are masters of their fates: The fault, dear Brutus, is not in our stars, but in ourselves, that we are underlings.

Cassius in Shakespeare, *Julius Caesar*

The Self and Control over Environment

Emerging from recent research and theorizing on the self-image of the black American is an important new dimension of self. This new dimension is the individual's perception of self as a locus of control over his environment. The importance of this personal control dimension for understanding the black self is enhanced by the peculiar position which blacks have occupied in American society.

Western culture generally and American culture particularly has relied extensively on the myth of potency to give meaning and direction to life (Ansbacher & Ansbacher, 1956). American society has been intensely preoccupied with the process of manipulating nature. That this preoccupation has had apparent payoff has been observed in the success of the physical sciences, agriculture, and industrialization. The frontier experience in America—economic, social, and geographical—also heightened the belief in the importance of individual potency as a valued personal attribute. On the frontier it seemed necessary that the individual be able to manage for himself. The belief that the individual alone was responsible for his success or failure became incorporated into the American cultural norm. The dissonance created by this dominant theme of self-potency, which permeates American culture and promotes a belief in the desirability, even the necessity, of being able to exert control over the environment, as against the prevailing realities surrounding the black man in American society makes this dimension of self-concept one of fundamental importance to blacks.

The central problem for the black self appears to be an undermining of the sense of responsibility. Certainly many blacks today (and this was true for even more in the past) are convinced that even if they assert their will, their actions will do no good. The critical problem, then, is this inner experience of impotence. The problem derives from the contradiction between the emphasis in American culture on the importance and necessity of power in the individual and the actual powerlessness of the black American. The black man, even if he knows who he is, may conclude he has no significance if he is unable to influence his environment.

Past analyses of identity among blacks have been unable to account for blacks' peculiar problems, primarily because such studies have not taken into account the role of intentionality and will as an essential means of expressing identity. The proposition of Descartes, "I think, therefore I am," on which much of our conceptualization of identity has been based, leaves out a significant variable. This proposition jumps from thought to identity with the intermediate variables of "I can" and "I will" being left out. Experience indicates that the correct sequence is "I think—I can—I will—I am" (May, 1969). "I can" and "I will" seem to be essential components of identity. Heider (1958) has also pointed out the contingency relations between *can* and *try* in the above paradigm. A person doesn't try if he doesn't believe he can. And, if this is his belief, then his identity must be profoundly affected.

The importance of this dimension of self has been reaffirmed recently by de Charms (1968), who has developed a motivational theory based on the proposition that man's primary motivational disposition is to produce changes in his environment. Thus, the person strives to be a causal agent, to be the origin of his behavior. The environment poses different problems, such as achieving economic security and gaining friendships; however, the fundamental personal dimension which underlies all of these environmental encounters is the attempt to overcome the problems through personal efficacy, to be the master of one's fate.

This analysis by de Charms elaborates upon Heider's (1944) notion of the person as an *origin* to develop the dimension of *origin-pawn*. This conceptual continuum, *origin-pawn*, seems to capture the basic notion to be discussed in this chapter as fundamental to an understanding of the black self. Although it is easy to convey the notion that some people conceive of themselves as masters of their fate, as *origins*, while others see themselves as *pawns* in the hands of fate, puppets on a string, this conception is far too simplistic and is distant from the realities of the matter. It is rather that the same person may feel more like a pawn under some circumstances and more in control of the situation in other circumstances. Not only is the feeling of self-control related to the situation, but there are also degrees of self-control rather than categorical "yes I am a pawn—no I am not a pawn" feelings.

Probably only the mentally ill are convinced absolutely that they are either origins or pawns. It is more likely that some degree of feeling along the continuum between these two extremes is the general rule. Within this continuum, general behavior patterns related to feelings of "self as an origin" versus "self as a pawn" can be predicted. Indeed, the practical significance of this *origin-pawn* dimension of self-concept relates to the way in which this dimension influences people's behavior. It has been generally observed that people who hold a strong belief in self as a pawn are relatively passive in any attempts to change the world. People who view themselves this way do not generally seek to better their positions or the conditions in which they find themselves. At the other end of the continuum, individuals who consider themselves as origins, as exerting personal control over the environment, are much more ambitious in their efforts to change the environment and the world around them. Frequently they are not merely ambitious but also creative, activist, and even revolutionary (Lefcourt, 1966a; Rotter, 1966).

What It Means to Be a Pawn

What does it mean when a person sees himself as a pawn, when he reports that he does not see himself as exerting control over his environment? He may believe this about himself for a number of different reasons—some realistic, some not. First, he may believe in luck or chance and conceive of the world as controlled by nondeterministic influences and therefore see it as unpredictable, both in terms of himself and others. Consequently, he cannot believe in his ability to influence events that happen to him, either good or bad. Merton (1949) has described belief in luck or chance as a type of defense mechanism designed "to serve the psychological function of enabling people to preserve their self-esteem in the face of failure." He further develops the relationship between the belief in luck and passivity. Historically, for the black American, this may have been one of the most useful and available psychological defense mechanisms to preserve self-esteem. To maintain mental health, some defense strategy of this type had to be employed, since frequently the only outcome for a black's efforts permitted by the dominant society was failure.

A second reason for seeing oneself as a pawn is a belief in fate. The person who attributes the things that happen to him to fate, asserts that the

course of events in the world have somehow been predetermined. The result is his inability to interfere with or change the course of these events. Although the belief in fate is frequently connected with religious beliefs, Veblen (1899) has pointed out how belief in fate and belief in luck or chance are closely related phenomena. Both result in a general passivity and a means of psychological defense in the face of defeat.

A third reason for an individual feeling he lacks control of events in his life is related to the first two but has a modern scientific outlook. He feels the world is too complex to permit prediction or control by an individual. This perhaps represents the educated man's view and can be observed in modern arguments regarding causality (Ryle, 1949).

Finally, the individual may see himself as a pawn because he sees the control of events in the world in the hands of others who hold immense power and who cannot be influenced by him, a powerless individual. This conception of a feeling of powerlessness at the hands of others who hold power is the interpretation that has been most widely discussed.

Conceptually, the basic notion underlying the idea of powerlessness is *alienation*. The notion of alienation, originating with the Marxist view of the worker's condition in a capitalist society, has perhaps the widest use of any concept in the social sciences today (Seeman, 1959). The Marxist notion was basically that the industrial worker had been excluded from the planning and decision making regarding his work and had consequently become engaged in an essentially uncontrollable activity where the decisions about him and his work were made by the entrepreneurs. As Gerth and Mills (1946) have shown, this notion of alienation as powerlessness was extended by Weber to include bureaucratic societies generally. More recently, Fromm's notion of an "escape from freedom" (Fromm, 1955) has set forth the thesis that faith in a "magic helper," an idealized, powerful leader, is also a response to feelings of alienation. Related to this thesis is the underlying proposition of Hoffer's popular work on *The True Believer* (1951), which also argues that it is the individual's need for a sense of power in conditions where he feels no sense of control that leads him to search for a "true" doctrine. In each of these analyses, alienation is seen as powerlessness, as a reason for the individual believing in the external control of events. The utility of such an interpretation is apparent. The condition of black Americans, from slavery to the present, has been fertile for the development of this feeling, just as was the condition of workers during the time of Marx. Indeed, if blacks have used this interpretation for their feelings of being pawns, it has surely been for the most part an accurate one.

Recent extensive research investigations of the concept of personal efficacy have been stirred by an analysis by Rotter (1966). Although Rotter's notions of "internal locus of control" versus "external locus of control" seem to parallel Heider's (1958) notion of "locus of causality" and de Charm's

(1968) notion of "origin-pawn," he derived his concept from a different source. Rotter derived the locus of control concept from social learning theory, and he uses the concept to refer to an individual's expectancy as to whether reinforcement can be obtained in particular situations. If a student in a classroom, for example, does not anticipate any contingency between his effort and the teacher's approval, then he may be said to hold an expectancy of *external* control of reinforcements. That is, there is no perceived relation between his action and the consequence. If, however, a student anticipates a direct relation between his effort and the teacher's approval, then he may be said to hold an expectancy of *internal* control of reinforcements. Thus, there is a perceived contingency between his actions and the consequences.

Rotter, Seeman, and Liverant (1962) have theorized that locus of control tends to generalize across a wide variety of situations, thus defining a major attribute of self—the degree to which the person believes he can or cannot control what happens to him. It is around this conception which research on the black self-image has revolved.

The Measurement of Locus of Control

Perhaps the principal reason why Rotter's work has stimulated the most research on the locus of control concept is because a major thrust of his work has been directed toward systematic measurement of the concept. The most widely used measure of locus of control was developed by Rotter and his associates and reported by Rotter (1966). The *Internal-External Locus of Control Scale* consists of 23 items. The following items are the most potent items in the scale. In each instance the *a* alternative represents external control.

25. a. Many times I feel that I have little influence over the things that happen to me.
    b. It is impossible for me to believe that chance or luck plays an important role in my life.
17. a. As far as world affairs are concerned, most of us are the victims of forces we can neither understand, nor control.
    b. By taking an active part in political and social affairs the people can control world events.
6. a. Without the right breaks one cannot be an effective leader.
   b. Capable people who fail to become leaders have not taken advantage of their opportunities.
18. a. Most people don't realize the extent to which their lives are controlled by accidental happenings.
    b. There really is no such thing as "luck."
16. a. Who gets to be boss often depends on who was lucky enough to be in the right place first.

> b. Getting people to do the right thing depends upon ability; luck has little or nothing to do with it.

11. a. Getting a good job depends mainly on being in the right place at the right time.
    b. Becoming a success is a matter of hard work; luck has little or nothing to do with it.

Similar scales have been developed to be used with children. Bialer (1961) developed a scale that could be answered "yes" or "no." Such items as these were included:

> Do you really believe a kid can be whatever he wants to be?
>
> When nice things happen to you, is it only good luck?
>
> When people are mean to you, could it be because you did something to make them mean?

Battle and Rotter (1963) developed a projective test called the "Children's Picture Test of Internal-External Control." This six-item cartoon test asks the child to indicate what he would say in various lifelike situations which involve attribution of responsibility—"Why does her mother always yell at her?"

Crandall, Katovsky, and Crandall (1965) developed the "Intellectual Achievement Responsibility Scale" which assesses children's beliefs concerning personal responsibility for their successes and failures in intellectual academic achievement situations. The following two items from this scale illustrate that the scale, unlike the others, focuses on situation-specific feelings of self-control. Again, in each instance, the *a* alternative is the external control choice.

> 2. When you do well on a test at school, is it more likely to be
>   (a) because the test was especially easy, or
>   (b) because you studied for it?
>
> 3. When you have trouble understanding something at school, is it usually
>   (a) because the teacher didn't explain it clearly, or
>   (b) because you didn't listen carefully?

Certainly, the outcome of an attempt to measure a psychological trait is always less than the intentional meaning of the trait on the conceptual level. That this is true for the internal-external control dimension of self-concept can be easily seen by a cursory examination of the illustrative items taken from the scales that psychologists have developed to measure this important dimension of self-concept. Nevertheless, for ideas to be put to the test of how well they fit events and conditions in the world, some mode of observation has to be developed, and these scales currently represent the best efforts of psychologists who have been doing research on this self-concept dimension. It is probably best to refer back to the actual scales when one is discussing the findings of particular research studies, since the actual scale reflects more than any other factor what was actually observed. It is for this reason that illustrative scale items which have been developed to measure the self-concept dimension of internal-external control have been included here.

Research on Personal Efficacy Among Blacks

The previous conceptual analysis of the internal-external control dimension (seeing oneself as an origin or a pawn) of self-concept indicated that when a person's access to valued societal goals has been limited or controlled by the larger society, then this person would normally be expected to develop a self-orientation reflecting external control. Truly, he is a pawn. Research evidence has consistently indicated that blacks score higher in an external control direction than do whites (Battle & Rotter, 1963; Lefcourt & Ladwig, 1965; Scott & Phelan, 1969; Coleman, 1966; Lefcourt & Ladwig, 1966). Furthermore, as might be expected, socioeconomic status also contributes to a person's feeling that he is a pawn (Franklin, 1966), with the result that lower-class blacks are more external in their views of self than either upper-class blacks or upper- or lower-class whites (Battle & Rotter, 1963).

From these research findings, it appears that belief in an external control of self is characteristic of groups that are marginal in American society. The history of black Americans contributes to our understanding of why a belief in external forces controlling the self is entirely reasonable. The status of blacks upon arrival in America, as slaves or chattels, did not permit them to be adequate cultural bearers. As people emerging from slavery they were especially vulnerable to the influence of the expectations of the majority, since the majority was the only group to which they could turn for an emulative reference group. Certain realities of the situation also contributed to the developing black self. Blacks were relatively far removed from sources of community power; they did not have access to educational, economic, and social opportunities; blacks could not, in general, participate fully in the dominant culture. These racial barriers, combined with their relatively low socioeconomic status, served to maintain a significant gap between the black minority and the white majority preventing adequate communication between them and understanding of the characteristics of each group by each other. When the minority tends to use the majority as an emulative reference group, as blacks have done, the result is usually that the minority tends to adopt those behaviors and beliefs about the self which they feel the majority holds to be desirable. The effect becomes a self-fulfilling prophecy, reinforcing the prejudiced feelings and beliefs of the majority (Merton, 1948). As Mead has emphasized, the self is "...essentially a social structure, and it arises in social experience. . .it is impossible to conceive of a self arising outside of social experience" (Mead, 1934). This notion, similar to Sullivan's idea of "reflected appraisals," in which the individual's self-appraisal arises out of what others think and feel about him (Cooley, 1902), suggests that self and its development is in the hands of "significant others" who communicate to the individual their appraisals of the individual which gradually become incorporated into the self. If the reflected appraisals of the individual's self reveal powerlessness and an inability to exert influence over his environment, then the individual would be expected to come to internalize this belief as a part of his self-image. Historically, the majority in America (the significant other) has reflected the image of powerlessness to blacks. In this way, the prejudices of the majority have been incorporated into the self-images of the minority (Merton, 1949).

Recent research lends considerable credence to this explanation. Studies of persons who suffered in Nazi concentration camps where the majority in control permitted essentially no opportunity for personal efficacy, reflecting to the prisoners their total dependence upon those in control for their survival, was that the prisoners became passive, childlike, and irresponsible, whereas they had been active and responsible people previous to being subjected to these conditions (Bettelheim, 1952). The "Sambo Image" described by Elkins (1963) appears to be related to the personal accommodation of blacks to both the expectancy of the majority regarding blacks and the lack of realistic opportunities for them to exercise personal efficacy. The "Sambo Image" as described by Elkins is as follows:

> Sambo. . .was docile but irresponsible, loyal but lazy, humble but chronically given to lying and stealing; his behavior was full of infantile silliness and his talk inflated with childish exaggeration. His relationship with his master was one of utter dependence and childlike attachment; it was indeed this childlike quality that was the very key to his being (Elkins, 1963, p. 82).

Elkins contends that the origins of the concentration camp type self-image and the Sambo self-image are the same. Both result from limited alternatives where there are few opportunities to exercise personal control, where dependence upon the powerful majority is expected, and where the image of the minority reflected by the majority is one of powerlessness. The most tragic effect in the long run is the ultimate attitude, "It doesn't matter." Unable to influence his environment, the individual becomes apathetic and then violent since inflicting pain (physical, mental, or economic) proves that he can influence somebody. Violence, directed outwardly or inwardly, is one way to overcome the frustrating and finally unendurable feeling of his own powerlessness.

Current studies of internal-external control, using questionnaire-type responses of blacks, have further contributed to the understanding of this dimension of the black self. Research findings indicate that it is necessary to distinguish between the belief that internal or external control operates generally in a society, an ideological belief, and the application of this belief to the individual's own self in his personal situation (Gurin, et al., 1969). To illustrate the point, there is a considerable difference between the following two items from Gurin's Internal-External Scales.

16. a. When I make plans, I am almost certain that I can make them work.
    b. It is not always wise to plan too far ahead because many things turn out to be a matter of good or bad fortune anyhow.
9. a. People will get ahead in life if they have the goods and do a good job; knowing the right people has nothing to do with it.
   b. Knowing the right people is important in deciding whether a person will get ahead.

Although, in both of these items, choosing the (a) response would indicate a belief in internal control, there seems to be a qualitative difference between endorsing items like number 9, which refer to people generally, and endorsing items like number 16, which refer specifically to self. Endorsement of items like number 16 reflect the belief which the person holds regarding his own self-competence, his ability to act as an origin rather than to personally respond as a pawn. In contrast, endorsement of items like number 9 seems to reflect the person's belief about the nature of the world generally. The point is that a person could believe in the ideology of internal control, rejecting the notion that luck, fate, or the complexity of the world determine success, while at the same time, believing that his own self is actually controlled by outside forces because of his own powerlessness.

The rationale developed earlier in the chapter certainly supports this hypothesis. Because they have historically relied on the majority white culture for emulation, blacks in America would be expected to have internalized the general cultural belief about internal control, yet they are painfully aware that these same beliefs cannot be applied to their personal life situations. White Americans, without having experienced discrimination and racial prejudice, would be less likely to perceive a dissonance between general cultural beliefs about internal-external control and what they have personally experienced. The Coleman study* (1966) also supports this notion. Coleman found that for black students, belief in internal control was the most important indicator of school achievement, in fact, twice as powerful a predictor of school achievement than any other variable studied. It is important to observe the nature of the questions asked by Coleman to

---

*One of the largest and most important educational research projects ever carried out in this country was the study of the equality of educational opportunity in U.S. Schools, sponsored by the federal government and directed by Dr. James S. Coleman.

ascertain belief in internal control. The predominant theme of the questions was what were the individual's perceptions of the particular situation in which he found himself and how much control did he feel that he personally had in his life situation. Items like "Every time I try to get ahead, something or someone stops me" and "People like me don't have much of a chance to be successful in life" call for a self-referent and seem to reflect the personal dimension more than an ideological dimension.

These research results indicate that if the concept of personal control is to be useful in understanding the black self, all referents must be to the personal life situation of the individual and not to life in general.

Personal Efficacy and the New Black Self

Internal control expectancies appear to be related to effective behavior in modern society (Lefcourt, 1966a). Blacks who consider themselves as origins are more likely to initiate and take an active part in activities designed to further civil rights (Gore & Rotter, 1963; Strickland, 1965). As has been previously noted, school achievment is highly related to this self-concept dimension (Coleman, 1966; Lessing, 1969; McGhee & Crandall, 1968). General achievement striving behavior such as the time spent in intellectual activities and the intensity of interest in academic pursuits is also closely correlated with perceived personal control (Crandall, Katkovsky, & Crandall, 1965; Crandall, Katkovsky, & Preston, 1962).

A number of other studies have indicated that persons who see themselves as pawns are more susceptible to manipulation from the outside (Getter, 1966; Strickland, 1970), especially to subtle manipulation (Gore & Rotter, 1963). These findings have considerable import for the general problem of mass persuasion and propaganda in an open society. Increasingly, in recent years, research studies have focused on the relation between the individual's perception of himself as a control agent in his environment and attempts to influence his life chances. It has been found, for example, that persons characterized as "internals" tend to know more about control-related information than persons characterized as "externals." Tuberculosis patients who were Internals know more about related health material than External TB patients did. Internals and Externals did not differ in their knowledge of neutral information (Seeman, 1963). Other studies have shown that internals are more likely to be civil-rights activists (Forward & Williams, 1970; Straits & Sechrest, 1963; James, Woodruff, & Werner, 1965), to be better able to stop smoking (Jones & Schrauger, 1968), to be better able to remedy their own personality problems (Phares, Ritchie, & Davis, 1968), to attempt to influence other people's opinions (Phares, 1965), and to practice some form of birth control (MacDonald, 1970). Also,

Internals are much more likely to resist attempts to influence them by outside sources. Presumably, such attempts to influence the Internal individual are viewed by him as inconsistent with his belief that he can exert control over his own environment. Consequently, he meets outside influences with resistance. The External, however, expects to be influenced by the environment and, consequently, he not only does not resist such outside influences, he tends to behave as expected. Ritchie and Phares (1969) have demonstrated that resistance to attempts to influence by Internals holds true not only for overt influence but for quite subtle influencing attempts as well.

More important for the black self are the implications of recent studies which have indicated that blacks who viewed their self-powerlessness to be due to conditions over which they could exert some influence are more likely to take personal action to bring about change in those conditions (Gurin, et al., 1969; Lao, 1970; Forward & Williams, 1970). If activism produces desirable change, then it would seem likely that the self-fulfilling prophecy could be reversed. Recent evidence does seem to indicate that this may be happening, at least in the context of schooling. One of the findings of the Coleman study (1966) was that, as the proportion of white students in a school increased, the sense of personal efficacy among black students became stronger. Black high-school seniors in the South who had attended segregated all-black schools (free choice) were more convinced of their self-powerlessness than were Southern black students who had attended desegregated high schools (no choice) (White, 1971). Both of these studies indicate that the black student who fights for and successfully encounters desegregated education, incorporates this experience into his self-conception of personal efficacy. Experiences such as these ought to weigh heavily on the future development of the black self.

Several recent studies have focused on child rearing practices that might be related to the development of a self-conception of personal efficacy. Research in this area is especially critical today with the development of public child-care facilities which have an awesome potential for influencing the self-concepts of children. At least one recent work has documented the immense influence that Soviet child-care facilities have apparently had on the personality of the Russian child (Bronfenbrenner, 1970). Research studies in America regarding child rearing practices and the development of a self-conception of efficacy have generally indicated that parent behaviors characterized as "warm," "praising," and "supportive" are positively associated with the development of feeling of internal control on the part of children, while parental behaviors characterized as "dominant," "rejecting," and "critical" were associated with the development of feelings of external control on the part of the children (Katkovsky, Crandall, & Good, 1967). The same study also suggested that the influence of the father's behavior and his relationships with his children may perhaps be a more potent source of influence on the development of feelings of self-efficacy than the influence of the mother. This finding takes on added importance when one considers the role of father absence on the development of the self-concepts of blacks. This is discussed in Chapter 2 from the child's perspective and in Chapter 4 from the point of view of the adult.

No direct relation has been observed between children's beliefs in self-efficacy and the parent's own belief in his or her self-efficacy (Davis & Phares, 1969). This evidence is encouraging since it suggests that a new generation can develop self-conceptions different from the older generation. With ever-increasing chances to influence the early development of children, from television to public child-care facilities, the importance of factors which will affect this dimension of self-image must be carefully evaluated. The evidence does seem to suggest that whether a person sees himself as a pawn or an origin has profound implications, not only for his own mental health and personal development but for the future of our society.

Black Power and the Development of Self-Efficacy

Accomplishments by black Americans in the past few years based upon self-initiated demands and action programs hold important implications for the development of self-efficacy. Black consciousness is rapidly being developed. Although the influence of this new black consciousness upon the young is not now known, it is clear that for many, if not most blacks in America, the traditional stereotype of the Sambo image has been rejected and in its place there is a positive stereotype—"black is beautiful." Thucydides said long ago that social revolutions occur when old terms take on new meanings. Perhaps the same can be said for personal revolutions concerning an individual's view of himself. Black has made a dramatic change from something that was bad, to be avoided, to a badge of intense pride that borders at times on racial superiority. Black power certainly signifies the ability to influence the environment. One interesting response to Black Power is the development of "reverse discrimination." Reverse discrimination is discrimination in favor of blacks. The practice of reverse discrimination means that blacks may be promoted, not because of skill or competence, but because they are black. In fact, some black spokesmen now demand this practice as a fundamental right. In many quarters today blacks are sought out and given preference over more qualified nonblacks. Those familiar with the situation know that both industry and colleges and universities are constantly recruiting blacks to meet some quota with little apparent regard for personal skill or competence in some cases.

These practices, in the long run, may be damaging to the black self in terms of the sense of personal control. Blacks will not be able to overlook the possibility that they may have been promoted in a discriminatory fashion, not unlike the discriminatory practices that resulted in their failure to be promoted in earlier times. Although the discrimination is in their favor economically, reverse discrimination does not give blacks consideration in terms of individual competence but rather as members of a group. It is a cruel irony that, as individuals, they may still have little or no control over the situation. Consequently, a highly qualified and competent black individual who is promoted to a high position cannot be certain whether he was promoted because of his ability and competence or because of his group membership. This practice could ultimately have the same consequences for the black's self-image of powerlessness as has the past practice of white racist discrimination in refusing to recognize the competence of blacks.

A concomitant effect of this reverse discrimination practice will be the psychological effect upon the white majority. Ultimately it may strengthen old prejudices, in that the white majority could come to see blacks as holders of positions for which they cannot legitimately qualify and in which they cannot adequately perform. Clearly, if the self-concept of the individual is to be strengthened relative to his ability to control his environment, discrimination by powerful elements in a society, either positive or negative, will be detrimental.

References

Ansbacher, H., & R. Ansbacher. *The individual psychology of Alfred Adler*. New York: Basic Books, 1956.

Battle, E., & J. Rotter. Children's feelings of personal control as related to social class and ethnic group. *Journal of Personality*, 1963, 31, 482-90.

Bettelheim, B. Individual and mass behavior in extreme situations. In G. Swanson, T. Newcomb, & E. Hartley (eds.), *Readings in social psychology*. New York: Holt, Rinehart & Winston, 1952.

Bialer, I. Conceptualization of success and failure in mentally retarded and normal children. *Journal of Personality*, 1961, 29, 303-20.

Bronfenbrenner, U. *Two worlds of childhood*. New York: Russell Sage Foundation, 1970.

Coleman, J. et al. *Equality of educational opportunity*. Washington, D.C.: U.S. Government Printing Office, 1966.

Cooley, C. *Human nature and the social order*. New York: Scribner's, 1902.

Crandall, V. C., W. Katovsky, & V. J. Crandall. Children's beliefs in their own control of reinforcement in intellectual-academic situations. *Child Development*, 1965, 36, 91-109.

Crandall, V. J., W. Katovsky, & A. Preston. Motivational and ability determinants of young children's intellectual achievement behaviors. *Child Development*, 1962, 33, 643-61.

Davis, W., & E. Phares. Parental antecedents of internal-external control of rein-forcement. *Psychological Reports,* 1969, 24, 427-36.

de Charms, R. *Personal causation.* New York: Academic, 1968.

Elkins, S. *Slavery.* New York: Grosset & Dunlap, 1963.

Forward, J., & J. Williams. Internal-external control and black militancy. *Journal of Social Issues,* 1970, 26, 75-92.

Franklin, J. *From slavery to freedom.* New York: Knopf, 1947.

Fromm, E. *The sane society.* New York: Holt, Rinehart & Winston, Inc., 1955.

Gerth, H., & C. Mills. *From Max Weber: Essays in sociology.* New York: Oxford University Press, 1946.

Getter, H. A personality determinant of verbal conditioning. *Journal of Personality,* 1966, 34, 397-405.

Gore, P., & J. Rotter. A personality correlate of social action. *Journal of Personality,* 1963, 31, 58-64.

Gurin, P., G. Gurin, R. Lao, & M. Beattie. Internal-external control in the motivational dynamics of Negro youth. *Journal of Social Issues,* 1969, 25, 29-53.

Heider, F. *The psychology of interpersonal relations.* New York: John Wiley, 1958.

Heider, F. Social perception and phenomenal causality. *Psychological Review,* 1944, 51, 358-74.

Hoffer, E. *The true believer.* New York: Harper, 1951.

James, W., W. Woodruff, & W. Werner. Effect of internal and external control upon changes in smoking behavior. *Journal of Consulting Psychology,* 1965, 29, 184-86.

Jones, S., & J. Schrauger. Locus of control and interpersonal evaluations. *Journal of Consulting and Clinical Psychology,* 1968, 32, 664-68.

Katovsky, W., V. C. Crandall, & S. Good. Parental antecedents of children's beliefs in internal-external control of reinforcements in intellectual achievement situations. *Child Development,* 1967, 38, 765-76.

Lao, R. Internal-external control and competitive and innovative behaviors among Negro college students. *Journal of Personality and Social Psychology,* 1970, 14, 263-70.

Lefcourt, H. Belief in personal control: Research and implications. *Journal of Individual Psychology,* 1966b, 22, 185-95.

Lefcourt, H. Internal versus external control of reinforcement: A review. *Psychological Review,* 1966a, 65, 206-20.

Lefcourt, H., & G. Ladwig. Alienation in Negro and white reformatory inmates. *Journal of Social Psychology,* 1966, 68, 153-57.

Lefcourt, H., & G. Ladwig. The American Negro: A problem in expectancies. *Journal of Personality and Social Psychology,* 1965, 1, 377-80.

Lessing, E. Racial differences in indices of ego functioning related to academic achievement. *Journal of Genetic Psychology,* 1969, 115, 153-57.

MacDonald, A., Jr. Internal-external locus of control and the practice of birth control. *Psychological Reports,* 1970, 27, 206.

May, R. *Love and will.* New York: Norton, 1969.

McGhee, P., & V. C. Crandall. Beliefs in internal-external control of reinforcements and academic performance. *Child Development,* 1968, 39, 91-102.

Mead, G. *Mind, self, and society.* Chicago: University of Chicago Press, 1934.

Merton, R. Social structure and anomie. In R. Merton (ed.), *Social theory and social structure.* Glencoe, Ill.: Free Press, 1949.

Merton, R. The self fulfilling prophecy. *The Antioch Review,* 1948, 8, 193-210.

Phares, E. Internal-external control as a determinant of amount of social influence exerted. *Journal of Personality and Social Psychology,* 1965, 2, 642-47.

Phares, E., E. Ritchie, & W. Davis. Internal-external control and reaction to threat. *Journal of Personality and Social Psychology,* 1968, 10, 402-5.

Ritchie, E., & E. Phares. Attitude change as a function of internal-external control and communicator status. *Journal of Personality,* 1969, 37, 429-43.

Rotter, J. Generalized expectancies for internal versus external control of reinforcement. *Psychological Monographs,* 1966, 80 (Whole No. 609).

Rotter, J., M. Seeman, & S. Liverant. Internal versus external control of reinforcements: A major variable in behavior theory. In N. Washburne (ed.), *Decisions, values, and groups,* Vol. 2. New York: Macmillan, 1962.

Ryle, G. *The concept of mind.* New York: Barnes & Noble, 1949.

Scott, J., & J. Phelan. Expectancies of unemployable males regarding source of control of reinforcement. *Psychological Reports,* 1969, 25, 911-13.

Seeman, M. Alienation and social learning in a reformatory. *American Journal of Sociology,* 1963, 69, 270-84.

Seeman, M. On the meaning of alienation. *American Sociological Review,* 1959, 24, 783-91.

Straits, B., & L. Sechrest. Further support of some findings about characteristics of smokers and non-smokers. *Journal of Consulting Psychology,* 1963, 27, 282.

Strickland, B. Individual differences in verbal conditioning, extinction, and awareness. *Journal of Personality,* 1970, 38, 364-78.

Strickland, B. The prediction of social action from a dimension of internal-external control. *Journal of Social Psychology,* 1965.

Swanson, G., T. Newcomb, & E. Hartley, eds. *Readings in social psychology.* New York: Holt, Rinehart, & Winston, 1952.

Veblen, T. *The theory of the leisure class.* New York: Macmillan, 1899.

Washburne, N., ed. *Decisions, values, and groups.* Vol. 2. New York: Macmillan, 1962.

White, K. Belief in reinforcement control among southern Negro adolescents: The effects of school desegregation, socioeconomic status, and sex of student. *Journal of Social Psychology,* 1971, 85, 149-50.

4

the social context of the black self

What white Americans have never fully understood—but what the Negro can never forget—is that white society is deeply implicated in the ghetto. White institutions created it, white institutions maintain it, and white society condones it.

Kerner Commission Report, 1968, p. 2

Although education may in the long run be an important instrument for black people, children may have clearer vision when they see the classroom as immediately irrelevant. Their vision is clearer than that of men who plead for black people to become educated in a land which views all blacks as bonds-men temporarily out of bondage. These are the poisonous waters through which black children must find their way.

W. H. Grier and P. M. Cobbs, *Black Rage,* p. 113

Time and knowledge must be turned toward understanding the course of socialization and affective development of Afro-American children, with Black self-perceptions being the dominant focus.

J. L. Johnson, Associate Superintendent of Schools, Washington, D.C.

Chapters 2 and 3 approached the black self largely from a developmental perspective. The role of the black family and its child-rearing practices, father-absence, the black community and its concomitant educational, social, and economic characteristics were discussed as antecedent conditions relating to the development of self-image. Black power and black powerlessness were presented as broad, often-discussed but seldom understood factors influencing real and perceived control over the individual's development of self. In this chapter we present research information and theoretical conceptions concerning the important social and behavioral correlates of self-image in black Americans. The purpose of the discussion is to help the reader view the black self-image as both cause *and* effect in studying black behavior.

For example, the family serves as a molder of self-identity on the one hand and is profoundly influenced by the images family members hold of themselves on the other. This circular characteristic of self-image can be illustrated by simply reversing many of the simplistic, stereotyped, cause-effect statements regarding black behavior. For example, the statement that "black men will never gain self-respect because they won't seek and hold decent jobs," becomes "black men won't seek decent jobs because they don't have enough self-respect." When the notion that "blacks don't improve their lot because they won't stay in school" is reversed, it reflects the reason many young blacks reject formal education and drop out of school. Of course, high unemployment and high school-dropout figures among blacks do not lend themselves to simple cause-effect statements of any type but are created by a crazy-quilt variety of many factors. It seems likely that the images each person holds of himself in different situations influences and, in turn, is influenced by family, marriage, employment, and personal-social adjustment generally. In this chapter we view these influences from the perspective of the adult.

Family and Marriage

The siren song of simple explanations for the high prevalence of broken families among blacks is seductive enough to have influenced the attitudes of the majority of Americans and even the legislation passed to comprehensively attack this problem and its effects. The cultural legacy of the black American simply does not provide him with the historical tradition of stable families and traditional marriages. Economic and social conditions emanating from the use of African slaves in the South have militated against the establishment of stable families governed by middle-class conventions. The modern black family, considerably more than its white counterpart, is plagued by disorganization. Beginning with the dissolution of the traditional African family during the American period of slavery to the mass ur-banization of blacks currently, black family life has been in a constant process of change, reacting to economic and social forces emanating from the larger society. Frazier (1957) presents evidence indicating that when black people achieve middle-class status, family stability becomes even more important than it is among the white middle class (pp. 82-83). The huge majority of black Americans are, of course, still found in the lowest socioeconomic status positions in society. Information from the U.S. Department of Labor (Bureau of Statistics) indicated that in 1970, nearly 27 percent of all black families in America were headed by a female as com-pared with 9 percent for whites.

The pattern of father-absent, mother-dominated homes and families has a long legacy. Slaves, being the property of slave holders, often did not develop family relationships because they could be, and frequently were, dissolved through the sale of one of the parties involved. Any children of a union of two slaves ordinarily remained with the mother. The American Civil War and the emancipation of slaves which followed it had a disturbing effect on whatever degree of stability slave families had managed to achieve. The general instability of the social order in the South following the Civil War was mirrored in increased instability among black families. Conditions conducive to the development of stable family relationships among blacks were not made any easier with the restoration of white supremacy in the South following the period of Reconstruction. The black man's self-image suffered further damage, and he found it even more difficult than he had as a slave to assume a position of dominance or even of equality with the black female following Reconstruction. The economic exploitation of black males during the beginning of the rural southern sharecropper economy, combined with the almost absolute social subordination of black males in the larger society, rendered him ineffective as a husband and father. These self-depreciatory conditions were made even more intolerable near the end of the 1800s with the passage of Jim Crow laws. Black men began to reject the rural southern environment at the beginning of the 1900s, and the period of black urbanization which continues to this day, began. The widespread and increasing migration of blacks from the rural south to urban slums did little to enhance the development of traditional family structure, organization, and values.

It should be noted here, however, that there is recent evidence which refutes the long-held assumption that the migration of Southern blacks to Northern cities is responsible for the high rates of inner-city unemployment and welfare. A report (1973) released by the U.S. Bureau of the Census showed that Southern-born black males have higher labor force participation than blacks born in the North. In New York City, for example, 78 percent of Southern-born black men 16 years and over who lived in the area in both 1965 and 1970 were employed in 1970, while only 65 percent of those born in New York state were employed at the time of the census.

Formal marriages, which were generally not permitted during the period of slavery, had only slightly more opportunity to develop during and immediately following Reconstruction. Earlier in the present century, when blacks lived primarily as rural agrarian people, the solution for the intolerability of a bad marriage was an easy one. The black man simply separated from the family with their knowledge and blessing, or he deserted them. Desertion and separation as the principal means of family dissolution among blacks followed lower-class blacks to the city and have continued.

The abandonment of the home by many black males affects a large number of children growing up in the racial ghetto (see Chapter 2). Most jobs available to lower-class black men are at the low end of the occupational scale, and these jobs usually lack the necessary status to sustain a worker's self-respect or the respect of his family and friends. Black men are bound to develop feelings of inadequacy arising from repeated failure to obtain and keep these jobs. Pettigrew (1964) documents the effects of family disorganization on the personalities of black children. Although the research evidence supporting relationships between black family disorganization and personality problems in black children and adults shows a wide variance in both quantity and quality, children from broken homes are more likely to develop personality problems than children from intact homes. The disproportionately high percentage of black children in America who grow up in broken homes was discussed in detail earlier (Chapter 2).

It may be too-often assumed that father-absent homes are ones in which fathers play little or no role in the rearing of the children. Most certainly, in some broken homes there may be no father-child relationship at all. In some cases, it is true that the father may not even know he is the father of the child; in others even the mother may not know who the father is. Viewing black father-absence globally, more typically we see a father-child relationship in which the father is separated from the child, acknowledges his paternity, admits to financial responsibility but is able to provide financial support only irregularly, if at all. His contacts with his child may be infrequent, irregular, and of short duration.

The Father-Child Relationship

The father-child relationship, more than the mother-child relationship, among blacks appears to be more influenced by such factors as the child's sex, skin color, and legitimacy. Drake and Cayton (1945) and Rosenberg (1965) report the tendency on the part of black fathers to clearly prefer a child with light skin who is legitimate. These authors also offer strong evidence that lower-class black fathers tend to be closer to their daughters than to their sons. Frazier (1957), in his study of the black family in the United States, also described the clear and sharp contrast between mother-son and father-son relationships.

In attempting to understand the role of self-concept upon family dynamics among black Americans, it may be helpful to remember that each individual family member develops and maintains his own concept of self. Each individual family member's self-concept is constantly influenced and restructured by its interaction with the self-concepts of others. For the young child, interaction with family members, particularly adults, is the only source of reflection as he develops his own concept of himself. An interesting facet of this situation appears when we look at black men as sons rather than as fathers. Here, the father-child relationship appears to be a considerably more distant one. In part, this may be due to the deterioration of the father-child relationship over time into the different assessments that father and son make of their relationship, each from his own point of view. When the child is very young, the father may still be living with the family or, in any case, making an attempt to support his family in some fashion. But after the father has left, as he often does, the growing distance in time and space between father and family makes it increasingly difficult to sustain even a semblance of family ties between the man, on one hand, and his wife and children on the other. Liebow (1967) reports that in casual conversation, black men seldom refer to their fathers spontaneously. A group of black men can reminisce for hours without the word being mentioned. The simple truth is that many black men never seemed to have really known their fathers. The cycle continued when these black men became fathers. Their own family experience as young boys and the families they observed as they grew up make it very difficult if not impossible, for many black men to develop adequate father roles.

Interestingly, considerably less is known about how the matriarchal model affects the self-concept of black women than about the attitudes, identities, and self-concept of black men and of black children. Very little is known, except by speculation, about the inner world of black women. The preoccupation with the dominant role of the black woman is largely due to growing concern over widespread social and psychological pathology among blacks. This appears to stem from psychological interpretations of ill effects, especially for males, of being reared in female-centered homes. Many of the factors which accompany the black family without a father—overcrowding, lack of privacy, noise, filth, disease—add their part to inadequate personal adjustment, lack of motivation, and the development of self-images among blacks which tend to be destructive rather than productive. The known and suspected effects of family and marital disorganization upon psychological and social adjustment are serious. Unfortunately, the maladjustment suffered by the individual is further reflected in the maladjustment of his environment. The black ghetto is most often a crime-ridden, violence-prone, poverty-stricken world. In such an environment, the image of a responsible husband and father, the educated young black, and that of the solid citizen is often not the image of success. Young blacks are acutely aware of a system which appears to offer rewards to those who illegally exploit others and failure to those who struggle under traditional responsibility. Under these circumstances, it is not surprising to find many bright, highly motivated young blacks adopting exploitation and the "hustle" as a way of life. The dope pushers and the numbers runners become the "successful" men because their earnings far outstrip those of the young people who try to climb the social and economic ladder in more conventional ways. This pattern has tended to reinforce itself from one generation to the next, creating a poverty culture and an ingrained cynicism about society and society's institutions. The next section of the chapter discusses the relationships between the black self and the behavioral disturbances and social maladjustments which have become a part of the black condition.

Behavioral Disturbances and Social Maladjustments

Hard data which illuminate the personal and social pathologies of the black self are not yet available in sufficient quantity and quality to be useful. Much of the information about the behavioral and social deviance traceable to the battered black self is statistical and not psychological. The report of the Kerner Commission (1968), for example, provided figures helpful in determining the extent of behavioral and social distress among black Americans. Somehow, as devastating as these figures are, they do not seem to increase the understanding of and the ability to provide resources for the individual black man, woman, and child. Pinkney (1969) has done an outstanding job of breathing life and meaning into the cold statistics concerning psychosocial deviance among blacks in the United States (pp. 120-38). In general, however, information about deviant behaviors and the black self which would be of most benefit to the helping professions has not come from systematic testing of theoretically based variables. Most available literature in this area is descriptive and is based on the less structured methods of sociologists and anthropologists. Psychologists have described certain positive features of self which allow individuals to cope. Murphy's research (1961) suggests that such behaviors as the ability to accept limits and resilience in mobilizing resources under stress are characteristic of young children who develop and maintain positive self-images. Kroeber (1963) identified a list of behaviors associated with successful defense of one's self-image: detachment, means-end symbolization, delayed response. The behaviors described as successful coping behaviors are, for the most part, the very behaviors which black children cannot and do not develop. In fact, lower-class black environments tend to produce children and youth who exhibit the exact opposite of many of these successful coping behaviors— inability to delay gratification, behavioral and conceptual impulsivity, inability to use verbal mediators to develop means-end symbolization, and poor attention.

Mental and Emotional Disorders

The black self which loses control (psychosis) or easily loses its stability (neurosis) has been studied both clinically and experimentally over the past thirty years (Faris & Dunham, 1939; Drake & Cayton, 1954; Malzberg, 1936, 1953; McClean, 1949; Eaton & Weil, 1955; Clark, 1959, 1965; Karlan, 1939; Frank, 1947; Dai, 1953; Williams & Carmichael, 1949; Pasamanick, 1962, 1963; Kardiner & Ovesey, 1962; Parker & Kleiner, 1966; Fantini & Weinstein, 1968; Halpern, 1970; Katz, 1969; Zirkel, 1971; and Bentz &

Edgerton, 1972). A review of the findings from this group of representative studies discloses a plethora of inconsistent and contradictory findings.

Pettigrew (1964), in his profile of the black American, seems to accept the common assumption that black people suffer disproportionately high rates of the more serious forms of mental illness. Pettigrew's assumption has the theoretical support of Merton (1957) and Durkheim (1951). Merton's sociological position promulgates the theory that goal-striving behavior may provide a focal breeding ground for various types of socially deviant and pathological reactions. The application of Merton's notion for the black American is that his social environment is one of depression, one characterized by caste barriers (both real and imagined), numerous social pressures, ambivalent identification, and status incongruity. These grossly deforming experiences differentially influence each individual black person, depending upon their particular combination and the circumstances. The social-psychological explanation of the relationships between self-image and psychopathologies is perhaps best exemplified by the theoretical and empirical work of Lewin (1935) and Festinger (1957). A principle American value supports the belief that the continually striving individual has a high probability of reaching his aspirations. Like his fellow Americans, the black individual internalizes these common success values and assumes that his chances of achieving his aspirations are also good. He too, is led to believe in the open social system which permits a high rate of social mobility. The bitter historical fact, however, is that the striving black has often been an exception to this American dream. It follows then, that his failure to achieve specific value goals causes him to perceive himself as a failure and to experience severe loss of self-esteem as a result.

Logical definitions of self emphasize the critical importance of social interaction with significant others. Whatever the specific antecedents are, low self-esteem has been found to characterize large numbers of black Americans, children and adults (Kardiner & Ovesey, 1951; Sclare, 1953). Even though the relationship between self-concept and ethnic group membership is not clearly predictable (Dreger & Miller, 1968; Katz, 1969), low and negative self-images appear to be crucial preconditions for mental disorder. Although studies in this area have utilized varying operational definitions of self-concept, the weight of the evidence establishing a direct relationship between negative self-image and poor mental health is impressive (Rogers, 1951; Calvin & Holtzman, 1953; Cowen, 1954; Rogers & Dymond, 1954; Combs & Syngg, 1959). Data have been reported which suggest that a simple and direct link between self-image and behavioral disturbance does not always exist. It has been found that in some instances groups categorized as maladjusted showed extremes of high and low self-esteem (Block & Thomas, 1955; Hatfield, 1958). McGinnies and Adornetto (1952) and Friedman (1955) found that some maladjusted patients characteristically repressed perceptions that could result in lowered self-esteem. The individual with an inadequate self-image may take great care to prevent further awareness of threats to his self-image. He finds that he can accomplish this end by perceptually distorting the reality of what he experiences. Combs and Snygg (1959) suggest that in the face of prolonged or severe threats to self, the individual may accept himself as defeated and incapable of dealing with life, and may readily acknowledge and even exaggerate his devalued self-image. Such reactions are common among psychotics.

The differential incidence of mental illness among blacks and whites based on available data is so contradictory, diverse, and conflicting as to make generalization tenuous, at best. The small amount of agreement among studies reporting incidence of mental illness indicates that blacks are more likely to suffer from such organic psychoses as general paresis, alcoholic psychoses, and from such functional psychoses as schizophrenia, particularly catatonic rather than paranoid or hebephrenic. In a recent study of the demographic correlates of psychiatric illnesses, Bentz and Edgerton (1972) reported that mental disorders were significantly higher among Southern rural blacks than among rural whites. Paranoid schizophrenia and manic-depressive psychoses would appear to be "white" mental illnesses, but Frazier (1957) and Schermerhorn (1956) indicate that when socioeconomic position is held constant, distinctions between black and white mentally ill persons in terms of types of disorders are essentially nonexistent.

Information on neuroses and the black self are less complete, probably because psychoses are more easily diagnosed, categorized, and certainly call more attention to themselves. Once again, the conflicting contributions of socioeconomic status and ethnic group membership cloud the picture. Since blacks are overrepresented among the poor and underrepresented among the middle class, it is not surprising to discover that a direct correlation between social class and the prevalence of neuroses has been found (Hollingshead & Redlich, 1958; Srole, 1962). The problem becomes one of determining why a disproportionate number of blacks as compared to whites suffer from more serious forms of mental illness. Is it because the black self is developed and must be maintained in an environment which interferes with nearly all forms of upward social mobility and, at the same time, limits other forms of acceptable self-expression? Or is it because data are more often reported for public than for private institutions, and, since black people are almost always treated in public mental institutions and almost never treated in private mental institutions, that the figures incorrectly represent the rate of severe mental illness among blacks?

Pinkney (1969) suggests that it is not meaningful to study mental and social deviance among black Americans unless the role of *discrimination* is added. Pinkney's discussion of social deviance and racism reflects a more modern view of the causes of social maladjustment. Two classic works (Frazier's *Black Bourgeoisie,* 1957, and Drake and Cayton's *Black Metropolis,* 1945), encouraged the conclusion that the plight of the black American could be traced to his historical and continuous condition of poverty. Moynihan (1965) indicates his belief that social scientists and laymen, black *and* white, have been too quick to blame deviant behavior on economic conditions. Moynihan suggests that the psychosocial damage to many black Americans may be of such magnitude that personal-social adjustment, even under the best of economic conditions, is virtually impossible. Kardiner and Ovesey (1962) and Douglass (1969) emphasize the importance of the combination and interaction of a host of factors, all of which affect blacks—low income, poor housing, lack of education, broken homes, discrimination, and segregation. Douglass comments that

> The central problem—to which all others are related—is that of racial discrimination, which psychologically, produces a self-image of low self-esteem as a result of the behavior and attitudes of whites toward him from childhood and its consequences for certain aspects of the Negro's ability to live at ease with his white fellowman (p. 349).

Grier and Cobbs's (1968) psychiatric work with blacks has led them to hypothesize that many of the behaviors of blacks which are labeled as deviant are, in fact, *adaptive,* and in some cases they are *survival* behaviors developed in response to the white environment.

Baughman's (1971) incisive description of "the white man's perspective" provides a means of understanding the black self. Using the concept of the *Black Norm,* developed by Grier and Cobbs (1968), Baughman urges his fellow psychologists to consider that many of the behaviors manifested by blacks are pathological only when judged by white standards. His message bears repeating here.

> These behaviors are simply adaptive devices developed in response to a peculiar environment.... They present normal devices for 'making it' in America and clinicians who are interested in the psychological functioning of black people must get acquainted with this body of character traits which we call the Black Norm. It is a normal complement of psychological devices, and to find the amount of sickness a black man has, one must first total all that appears to represent illness and then subtract the Black Norm. What remains is illness and a proper subject for therapeutic endeavor. To regard the Black Norm as pathological and attempt to remove such traits by treatment would be akin to analyzing away a hunter's cunning or a banker's prudence. This is a body of characteristics essential to life for black men in America and woe be unto that therapist who does not recognize it (p. 70).

To discuss abnormality and deviance is to assume comparison with some standard of normality. Unless the black individual can be viewed within his own frame of reference, his behavior cannot be accurately assessed with regard to its normality or abnormality. The clinical and psychiatric professional training programs in the United States must produce persons who are capable of properly diagnosing and treating emotional disturbances among minority group individuals. Clinicians and their teachers must discontinue the practice of applying white norms to label and stigmatize blacks who developed these behaviors in reaction to the exclusion and discrimination forced upon their culture by a white society.

Social Deviance

Whites seem to find it easier to understand and identify with the black who becomes mentally or emotionally ill than the black who robs, rapes, or riots. Yet, the same intense, oppressive conditions which create one can and do create the other.

The figures are everywhere. They are collected annually by the FBI; they are reported each ten years as part of the nation's census data; they are bandied about by a dizzying array of federal and state commissions and legislative hearings on crime, delinquency, health care, drug abuse, welfare reform, urban renewal, better schools, and so on, *ad nauseum*. Regardless of the statistical inaccuracy which surrounds and confuses these figures, one fact stands out clearly—black Americans show a disproportionate degree of deviance from the social and legal norms of American society. No purpose will be served here by presenting another collection of the statistics on crime and delinquency among blacks. Figures are available in the latest edition of *Uniform Crime Reports* compiled by the U.S. Department of Justice. The Kerner Commission Report (1968) is a good, though somewhat less official, source of information on the prevalence of social deviance among black Americans.

A "miniculture" which has attracted much attention from police and from the mass media is the black street culture. Horton's (1970) outstanding skill at observing and describing this miniculture provides added meaning to Baughman's plea for ethical therapeutic intervention which was discussed earlier in connection with emotional deviance. Over a two-year period, Horton observed and interviewed 25 young (ages 18 to 25) blacks who were members of the street culture. By middle class standards they were considered "unemployed hoodlums" and were engaged in social deviance such as theft, prostitution, drug traffic, illegitimacy, vagrancy, and public intoxication. Horton contends that such behaviors may be morally and legally wrong, but for these young blacks, such behaviors are rationally right. These same young blacks could not succeed educationally or vocationally; only four of the 25 were high school graduates and none held steady employment. They could not succeed in middle class schools and they could not succeed in the middle class job market because their assets were turned into liabilities in these settings. In the street, they can do those things they do best and are rewarded, materially and socially, for it.

The Black Self in School

Until the middle of the twentieth century, public education in the United States was our most popular religion. From the earliest days of this nation's birth, education was the unquestioned path to upward mobility for its people. Yet, once this grand old maiden finally relinquished her pristine status, even education's most ardent suitors admitted her numerous faults and weaknesses. There has been an avalanche of critical books and articles since the first broad attacks on schools decrying the irrelevance, ineffectiveness, and incompetence of public education. Educational philosophers began to find their arguments over whether schools lead social change or whether education reflects the existing social order falling on deaf and uncaring ears. The ability of public education to meet the demands of its consumers began to falter when the system (or nonsystem) could no longer adapt to rapidly occurring variations and shifts in jobs, population, technology, communications, social and geographic mobility, wealth and poverty. Realization of the American dream through public education must seem like a sick joke to young blacks who find, as Goodman (1964) describes, that

> Negro college graduates average in a lifetime the same salary as white high school graduates. After seven or eight years, the salary increase of Negro and Puerto Rican high school graduates over those who have dropped out is perhaps $5 a week. Is this worth the painful effort of years of schooling that is intrinsically worthless and spirit-breaking?

Despite the criticisms of public education, whether from scholarly, informed critics or from pseudo-intellectual doomsayers, the greatest gains in the U.S. socioeconomic strata recently made by black Americans have been in education. Mack's (1970) figures indicate that between 1960 and 1969 the percentage of eighteen- and nineteen-year-old black youths enrolled in U.S. schools increased from 35 percent to 45 percent, and that the percentage of black high school graduates increased during the same decade from 36 percent to 60 percent (p. 9). Figures for whites were considerably less exciting (63 percent to 78 percent). These gains say nothing about *what* public education is doing to increase its apparent attractiveness to young blacks, only that, paradoxically, its holding power is at its highest peak at a point in time when the reputation of schools is at, perhaps, its lowest ebb.

This particular paradox is reflected by a broader incongruity which causes confusion and frustration among most observers of the current social order. The more gains black Americans achieve in the arenas of education, economics, and politics, the higher the level of dissatisfaction grows and the more insistent their demands become. Many Americans who supported the right of black citizens to move to the front of the bus in the 1960s felt they could reasonably expect the 1970s to bring a lessening of demands for access to middle-class America. Highly visible examples of progress and opportunity were shown to blacks in the late 1950s and early 1960s, but they did not provide the expected safety valve to reduce pressure. Instead, there was increased pressure for equality and more widespread intolerance to racial discrimination. White Americans who supported the early civil rights movement with their minds, found their hearts joining the Silent Majority. These Americans forgot a most important lesson of history; revolutionary movements are led by intelligent, dedicated people who have a reasonable hope of improving their life chances, not by those who have given up. Slaveowners and Klansmen from earlier times and the rednecks and "Archie Bunkers" of more recent times predicted what has come to threaten the jobs, schools, ballotboxes, and neighborhoods of the Silent Majority. The states which passed laws during the slave period making it illegal to educate blacks knew the importance of enslaving the intellect as well as the body. Violations of these laws, particularly by small planters, were apparently quite common, and many instances of slaveowners teaching their slaves to read and write have been documented.*

Danger to the existing social order comes, not from people who accept the abject hopelessness of serfdom and slavery, but from serfs and slaves who have had their minds expanded by literacy and learning. The American black movement was and is led, not by illiterate shufflers, hanky-heads, and Uncle Toms, but by well educated black clergymen, professors, lawyers, writers, and students. Is it any wonder that Pearl and Riessman (1965) refer to education as "the complicated, the ultimate, and the enigmatical solution"?

The fact that lack of education and conditions of poverty are coexisting components in the life spaces of most blacks does not mean that poor blacks

*The reader who wishes to study further the educational history of black Americans will find several older, but excellent sources as well as more recent works on this topic. See Carter G. Woodson, *The Education of the Negro Prior to 1861* (New York: G. P. Putnam's Sons, 1919); Horace M. Bond, *Education of the Negro in the American Social Order* (New York: Prentice-Hall, 1934); John Hope Franklin, *From Slavery to Freedom* (New York: Knopf, 1947); W. A. Low, "The Education of Negroes Viewed Historically," in V. A. Clift, et al. (eds.), *Negro Education in America* (New York: Harper & Row, 1962); Virgil A. Clift, "Educating the American Negro," in J. P. Davis (ed.), *The American Negro Reference Book* (Englewood Cliffs, N.J.: Prentice-Hall, 1966); H. S. Ashmore, *The Negro and the Schools* (Chapel Hill, N.C.: University of North Carolina Press, 1954).

are poor simply because they are uneducated. It is generally accepted that the three most reliable indicators of status in our society are *education, occupation,* and *income,* but the nature of the interrelationships among these factors is dynamic, not static. Any fool can see that one's level of education largely determines the types of occupations available to him and, in turn, that one's occupation is clearly related to his level of income. Therefore (the fool reasons), the solution to the reduction and eradication of poverty and its apocalyptic side-effects is education. It may be that the massive steps taken over the past decade have, to some extent, followed such a simplistic line of reasoning—the Economic Opportunity Act of 1964, welfare reform, school desegregation, and system-wide bussing of pupils are prime examples. Reforms in the social system that relegate blacks to a subordinate status have been internal (federal legislation and court decisions) and external (civil rights leadership, black revolutionary influences). Regardless of their gaps and inadequacies, these reforms have had a positive impact on the lives of black Americans. No doubt, some blacks feel as Bayard Rustin (1971) does, that civil rights and antipoverty programs have made no significant, visible change in the black American's life. Survey research data reported by Brink and Harris (1967) prior to the time of Rustin's remarks, however, indicated that black respondents overwhelmingly thought that their lives had been bettered in recent times. Sixty-seven percent reported that "compared with three years ago, things are better off for me and my family"; five percent said, "worse."

The school, in which attendance is compulsory, is still this society's one and only access point to *all* of its children. The school, despite its tarnished image, is still looked upon by Americans as the process most uniquely qualified to prepare children to function in a society propelled by advancing technology. Perhaps the intense heat created by school desegregation, bussing, and racial balancing has kept sufficient light from being focused on the individual child, his school-related experiences, and his self-image. Public education for most black children is often said to be irrelevant and meaningless. The lack of meaning in the educational experience of black pupils is bound closely with the general ignorance concerning the educational implications of the psychology of the black self. In fact, Jersild (1965) contends that the search for meaning is essentially a search for self. He suggests that, "The crucial test in the search for meaning in education is the personal implication of what we learn and teach." Educators must build bridges between the mind and the heart in order to help black pupils understand how what they are learning relates to them as individuals. School learning for black children cannot be effective as long as educators assume that information and skills have value apart from their meaning for those who acquire this knowledge.

Self-Concept and Learning Problems

There seems to be increased interest in the crucial role of feelings about self in the learning process. Attempts to develop learning environments for disadvantaged children, however, have tended to revolve around cognitive adaptations. The rationale is simple: these children are handicapped in the fundamental *learning skills,* therefore programs must be developed that will reduce or eliminate these *learning deficits.* Psychologists and educational researchers have produced a convincing body of empirical data which indicates that for lower-class black children (as well as other groups of lower-class, disadvantaged children), learning problems stem as much from *motivational* factors as from *cognitive* factors. MacMillan (1971) provides three salient examples of motivational and emotional variables which depress the school performance of black pupils *below* their level of measured intellectual potential:

1. *Expectancy for failure.* Note the distinction between *fear* of failure and *expectancy* of failure. The goal of the black pupil may become one of protecting his self-image from further damage by working to avoid failure rather than striving to achieve success.
2. *Positive and negative reaction tendencies.* Zigler (1966) called the desire to interact with an approving adult the "positive reaction tendency," and the wariness toward adults as the "negative reaction tendency." It is likely a safe conjecture that when a black pupil is confronted with a white teacher, the child displays an even greater amount of mistrust, perhaps fear. The threat to the child's self is perceived by him as imminent, and he is able to devote little time and attention to academic learning tasks.
3. *Outerdirectedness.* Pupils who enter a learning situation with basic learning deficits quickly find that their responses and solutions are often wrong. Therefore, they tend to seek external cues, guides, and evaluations; such behavior is the exact opposite of the usual tendency for children to develop increased innerdirectedness as they mature and learn to trust internal, more abstract processes.

Research evidence which supports the significant relationship between self-image and school achievement is overwhelming.* A point of caution should be entered here because of recent findings regarding the influence of the civil rights movement on the black self (Halpern, 1970; Roth, 1970). Kvaraceus (1965) pointed out that our ideas concerning the influence of skin

*P. B. Campbell, 1967, "School and Self-Concept," *Education Leadership,* 24: 510-15; J. Bledsoe, 1967, "Self-concept of children and their intelligence, achievement, interests, and anxiety," *Childhood Education,* 43: 436-38; W. B. Brookover and S. Thomas, 1963, "Self-concept of ability and school achievement," *Sociology of Education,* 37: 271-75; M. D. Coplin, 1968, "Self-concept, level of aspiration, and academic achievement," *Journal of Negro Education,* 27: 435-39; E. G. Epps, 1969, "Correlates of academic achievement among northern and southern urban negro students," *Journal of Social Issues,* 25: 55-70; P. A. Zirkel, 1971, "Self-concept and the disadvantage of ethnic group membership and mixture," *Review of Educational Research,* 41: 211-25.

color on personality may be changing as a result of the Black Movement and the Afro styles which it has spawned.

John L. Johnson (1971) takes a strong position on the importance of focusing upon self-enhancement for the black pupil: "Time and knowledge must be turned toward understanding the course of socialization and affective development of Afro-American children, with black self-perceptions being the dominant focus" (p. 378).

References

Ashmore, H. *The Negro and the schools.* Chapel Hill: University of North Carolina Press, 1954.

Baughman, E. *Black Americans: A psychological analysis.* New York: Academic, 1971.

Bentz, W., & J. Edgerton. Demographic correlates of psychiatric illness. *Research Previews,* 1972, 19, 7-13. (Institute for Research in Social Science, University of North Carolina, Chapel Hill.)

Block, J., & H. Thomas. Is satisfaction with self a measure of adjustment? *Journal of Abnormal and Social Psychology,* 1955, 51, 254-59.

Bond, H. *Education of the Negro in the American social order.* Englewood Cliffs, N.J.: Prentice-Hall, 1934.

Brink, W., & L. Harris. *Black and white: A study of U. S. racial attitudes today.* New York: Simon & Schuster, 1967.

Calvin, A., & W. Holtzman. Adjustment and the discrepancy between self-concept and inferred self. *Journal of Consulting Psychology,* 1953, 17, 39-44.

Caplan, G., ed. *Prevention of mental disorders in children.* New York: Basic Books, 1961.

Clark, K. Color, class, personality and juvenile delinquency. *Journal of Negro Education,* 1959, 28, 240-51.

Clark, K. *Dark ghetto.* New York: Harper & Row, 1965.

Clift, V. Educating the American Negro. In J. Davis (ed.), *The American Negro reference book.* Englewood Cliffs, N. J.: Prentice-Hall, 1966.

Clift, V., et al., eds. *Negro education in America.* New York: Harper & Row, 1962.

Combs, A. & D. Snygg. *Individual behavior.* (2nd ed.) New York: Harper & Row, 1959.

Dai, B. Some problems of personality development among Negro children. In C. Kluckhohn & H. Murray (eds.), *Personality in nature, society, and culture.* New York: Knopf, 1953.

Davis, J., ed. *The American Negro reference book.* Englewood Cliffs, N.J.: Prentice-Hall, 1966.

Douglass, J. The urban Negro family. In J. Davis (ed.), *The American Negro reference book.*

Drake, S., & H. Cayton. *Black metropolis.* New York: Harcourt Brace, 1945.

Dreger R., & K. Miller. Comparative psychological studies of Negroes and whites in the United States: 1959-1965. *Psychological Bulletin Monograph Supplement,* 1968, 70, No. 3, Part 2.

Durkheim, E. *Suicide.* Translated by J. Spaulding and G. Simpson. Glencoe, Ill.: The Free Press, 1951.

Eaton, J., & R. Weil. *Culture and mental disorders.* New York: Free Press, 1955.

Ellis, N., ed. *International review of research in mental retardation.* Vol. 1. New York: Academic, 1966.

Endo, R., & W. Strawbridge, eds. *Perspectives on black America.* Englewood Cliffs, N.J.: Prentice-Hall, 1970.

Fantini, M., & G. Weinstein. *The disadvantaged.* New York: Harper & Row, 1968.

Faris, R., & H. Dunham. *Mental disorders in urban areas.* Chicago: University of Chicago Press, 1939.

Festinger, L. *A theory of cognitive dissonance.* Evanston, Illinois: Row, Peterson, 1957.

Frank, J. Adjustment problems of selected Negro soldiers. *Journal of Nervous and Mental Disorders,* 1947, 105, 647-60.

Franklin, J. *From slavery to freedom.* New York: Knopf, 1947.

Frazier, E. *Black bourgeoisie.* Glencoe, Ill.: Free Press, 1957.

Friedman, I. Phenomenal, ideal, and projected concepts of self. *Journal of Abnormal and Social Psychology,* 1955, 51, 611-15.

Goodman, P. Don't jail the young. *American Child,* 1964, 46, 3-7.

Grier, W., & P. Cobbs. *Black rage.* New York: Basic Books, 1968.

Halpern, F. Self-perception of black children in the civil rights movement. *American Journal of Orthopsychiatry,* 1970, 40, 520-26.

Hamachek, D., ed. *The self in growth, teaching, and learning.* Englewood Cliffs, N.J.: Prentice-Hall, 1965.

Hatfield, J. A study of self-concept configurations in relation to forms of ego functioning. Unpublished doctoral dissertation, University of California at Berkeley, 1958.

Hollingshead, A., & F. Redlich. *Social class and mental illness.* New York: John Wiley, 1958.

Horton, J. Time and cool people. In R. Endo & W. Strawbridge (eds.), *Perspectives on black America.*

Jersild, A. D. The search for meaning. In D. Hamachek (ed.), *The self in growth, teaching, and learning.*

Johnson, J. Special education in the inner city. In R. Jones (ed.), *Problems and issues in the education of exceptional children.* Boston: Houghton-Mifflin, 1971.

Jones, R., ed. *Problems and issues in the education of exceptional children.* Boston: Houghton-Mifflin, 1971.

Kardiner, A., & L. Ovesey. *The mark of oppression.* New York: World, 1962. (Paperback)

Karlan, S. A comparative study of psychoses among Negroes and whites in the New York State prison. *Psychiatric Quarterly,* 1939, 13, 160-64.

Katz, I. A catalog of personality approaches to Negro performance with research suggestions. *Journal of Social Issues,* 1969, 30, 13-28.

Keogh, B., & D. MacMillan. Effects of motivational and presentation conditions on digit recall of children of differing socioeconomic, racial, and intelligence groups. *American Educational Research Journal,* 1971, 8, 27-38.

Kluckhohn, C., & H. Murray, eds. *Personality in nature, society, and culture.* New York: Knopf, 1953.

Kroeber, T. The coping functions of ego mechanisms. In R. White (ed.), *The study of lives: essays on personality in honor of Henry A. Murray.* New York: Atherton, 1963.

Kvaraceus, W. Is there a new Negro? In W. Kvaraceus, et al. (eds.), *Negro self-concept: implications for school and citizenship.* New York: McGraw-Hill, 1965.

Lewin, K. *A dynamic theory of personality.* Translated by D. Adams and K. Zener. New York: McGraw-Hill, 1935.

Liebow, E. *Tally's corner.* Boston: Little, Brown, 1967.

Low, W. The education of Negroes viewed historically. In V. Clift, et al. (eds.), *Negro education in America.*

McGinnies, E., & J. Adornetto. Perceptual defense in normal and in schizophrenic observers. *Journal of Abnormal and Social Psychology,* 1952, 47, 833-37.

Mack, R. (ed.) *Prejudice and race relations.* Chicago: Quadrangle Books, 1970.

MacMillan, D. Special education for the mildly retarded. In R. Jones (ed.), *Problems and issues in the education of exceptional children.*

Malzberg, B. Mental disease among Negroes in New York State. *Mental Hygiene,* 1953, 37, 450-76.

Malzberg, B. Migration and mental disease among Negroes in New York State. *American Journal of Physiological Anthropology,* 1936, 21, 107-13.

McClean, H. The emotional health of Negroes. *Journal of Negro Education,* 1949, 18, 283-90.

Merton, R. *Social theory and social structure.* Glencoe, Ill.: Free Press, 1957.

Moynihan, D. Employment, income, and the ordeal of the Negro family. *Daedalus,* Fall, 1965, 758-69.

Murphy, L. Preventive implications of development in the preschool years. In G. Caplan, (ed.), *Prevention of mental disorders in children.*

Parker, S., & R. Kleiner. *Mental illness in the urban Negro community.* New York: Free Press, 1966.

Pasamanick, B. Some misconceptions concerning differences in racial prevalence of mental disease. *American Journal of Orthopsychiatry,* 1963, 33, 72-86.

Pasamanick, B. A survey of mental disease in the urban population. *American Journal of Psychiatry,* 1962, 119, 299-305.

Pearl, A., & F. Riessman. *New careers for the poor.* New York: Free Press, 1965.

Pettigrew, T. *A profile of the Negro American.* Princeton, N.J.: Van Nostrand, 1964.

Pinkney, A. *Black Americans.* Englewood Cliffs, N.J.: Prentice-Hall, 1969.

Report of the National Advisory Commission on Civil Disorders (Kerner Commission Report). Washington, D.C.: U.S. Government Printing Office, 1968.

Rogers, C. *Client centered therapy.* Boston: Houghton-Mifflin, 1951.

Rogers, C., & R. Dymond. *Psychotherapy and personality change.* Chicago: University of Chicago Press, 1954.

Rosenberg, M. *Society and the adolescent self-image.* Princeton, N.J., Princeton University Press, 1965.

Roth, R. How Negro fifth grade students view black pride concepts. *Integrated Education,* 1970, 8, 24-27.

Rustin, B. A way out of the exploding ghetto. *New York Times Magazine,* August 13, 1967.

Schermerhorn, R. Psychiatric disorders among Negroes: A sociological note. *American Journal of Psychiatry,* 1956, 28, 112-18.

Sclare, A. Cultural determinants in the neurotic Negro. *British Journal of Medical Psychology,* 1953, 26, 278-88.

Srole, L. *Mental health in the metropolis: The mid-town Manhattan study.* New York: McGraw-Hill, 1962.

U.S. Census Bureau Report, "Selected Social Characteristics of Southern and Northern-Born Blacks," July 1973.

U.S. Department of Labor, Bureau of Labor Statistics, "Black Americans: A Chartbook," 1971, Bulletin No. 1699, U.S. Government Printing Office.

White, R., ed. *The study of lives: essays on personality in honor of Henry A. Murray.* New York: Atherton, 1963.

Williams, E., & C. Carmichael. The incidence of mental disease in the Negro. *Journal of Negro Education,* 1949, 18, 276-82.

Woodson, C. *The education of the Negro prior to 1861.* New York: G. P. Putnam's Sons, 1919.

Zigler, E., & E. Butterfield. Motivational aspects of change in IQ test performance of culturally deprived nursery school children. *Child Development,* 1968, 39, 1-14.

Zigler, E. Research in personality structure in the retardate. In N. Ellis (ed.), *International review of research in mental retardation.* Vol. 1.

Zirkel, P. Self-concept and the disadvantage of ethnic group membership and mixture. *Review of Educational Research,* 1971, 41, 211-25.

5

the future
of
the black self

I was born black, poor, and uneducated, and you only need three strikes all over the world to be out.... I have nothing to live for but this shot of dope.... Your environment, I read somewhere, is just a mirror of yourself, so what can I do?... I don't think I could be rehabilitated, you know, not now, in this society.

Quoted in Kenneth B. Clark, *Dark Ghetto,*
New York: Harper & Row, 1965, pp. 95-97.

...if enough people believe a doctrine of racial inferiority for long enough, the doctrine itself will have consequences whether or not it is factually true. If Negroes are inferior, it is a waste of money to try to educate them at the same level as whites. If one believes this, then it is sensible to allocate less money to Negro schools and to be satisfied with inferior facilities, teacher training, and curricula. The vicious circle is closed when the products of this educational system turn out to score lower on IQ and achievement tests than white students. The end product of the prophecy that Negroes are inferior becomes evidence for the inferiority of Negroes. The prophecy becomes the condition.

Raymond W. Mack, *Prejudice and Race Relations,*
Chicago: Quadrangle Books, 1970, p. 107.

Being black in America is first of all being; it is existing. The key, however, is *becoming;* becoming points toward the future. The major concern for black Americans in the days to come must be the continued recovery of black identity. Because of the powerlessness experienced by blacks in American society for so long, self-survival and self-determination have been the goals pursued by black people—not self-realization. Few people in the world are unaware of the widespread dissatisfaction of black Americans. It is basically a dissatisfaction with the black self as it has been. It reflects the stirrings of a new search for self which is manifested in black literature, music, art, cinema, and drama. These expressions reflect the black self as never before in the history of the black American, and it is likely that the best is yet to come. The new black self is no longer being—it is becoming. Perhaps the principal reason why this fundamentally important facet of the Movement will succeed is that, finally, black people are beginning to define self in black terms.

The rationale for Jerome Bruner's "essays for the left hand" (*On Knowing,* 1963) provides a frame of reference through which the reader might approach this chapter. Bruner characterizes the right hand as the representative of order, system, science, and action. The left hand symbolizes sentiment, intuition, art, and even fantasy. It is Bruner's contention that in the behavioral scientist's drive to be recognized as a disciplined and systematic knowledge seeker, he has overlooked the fact that "...the great hypotheses of science are gifts carried in the left hand" (Bruner, 1963, p. 2).

Much of what is described and discussed in this chapter has been subjectively sought and grasped by the left hand. Unlike the strong, often unbending right hand, the left hand is awkward but supple, undisciplined but creative. Perhaps only such a hand can capture many of the elusive and unwieldy problems which confront man today. Surely, it is not sufficient to simply catch and hold problems so as to observe them more closely. But, by use of the left hand in this manner, perhaps we can "...tame them in the sense of shifting them from the left hand to the right hand by rendering them into notions that can be tested" (Bruner, p. 4).

Theoretical Considerations

The interpersonal theory of Sullivan (1953) is particularly relevant to the black American experience and speaks directly to what may be expected in the future. This theoretical frame of reference permits the isolation of key determinants of self for close observation and analysis, a task which is necessary if an understanding is to be gained of what the future holds for the black self. Briefly, Sullivan's contention is that the estimations and expectations of *others* provide the key to unlocking most doors to an adequate understanding of self. Further, the majority of "others" can, for all practical purposes, be neglected. Those others who are *significant* are the ones who count. Sullivan developed this notion of *significant others* from Mead's earlier conception of the generalized other, i.e., the social group or organized community which gives the individual his unity of self (Mead, 1934).

In order to be significant, others must hold, or be believed to hold, influence over an individual's personal situation. Within this context the possibilities for self-concept change are great—change directed for either benevolent or malevolent ends. If the development and maintenance of certain self-conceptions are, as Sullivan proposes, dependent upon support of *significant others*, the individual would expect to be able to alter self. This can be done and, in fact, is being done with rather impressive results among black people who have focused on "black consciousness." Until recently, the black self has been conceptualized almost exclusively in terms of the white self. Most research studies have involved a comparison of self-concepts of blacks with self-concepts of whites, the implication being that the white self is or ought to be the significant other. It has apparently not crossed the minds of most social scientists that an obvious research topic should be aspects of self-concept within the black personality and within the black community.

The New Black Self

The emphasis on black consciousness and the unique qualities of blackness signal a changing of the mirror in which self will be reflected. The "black is beautiful" theme is sometimes seen as a by-product of the headline-getting political and economic thrusts of the Black Movement. It is much more likely that the new black self is the real driving force of the Movement rather than a spin-off. It is revealing to look backward at Malcolm X from the objective distance of a decade in attempting to chart the future course of the black self. His writings (1965) indicate a clear insight into an understanding that black power begins with the individual black American. He consistently pressed forward the concept of positive identification. This man knew from his own experience of slum life and from the depths of his own blackness that any black person who believes that he cannot influence the direction of his own life as an individual, can never influence the destiny of black Americans as a group.

The shift away from attempts to mask blackness with skin bleaches and hair straighteners toward attempts to express, even flaunt, blackness represents much more than superficial and cosmetic appearance. It represents a major change in the fiber from which the new black self is woven. The significant other for many black people in America today has shifted from the middle-class white stereotype to black role models who are significant *in their own terms*. In his book, *Who Speaks for the Negro*, Warren (1966) records the following true incident which dramatically depicts the new black self:

> ...The auditorium had been packed—mostly Negroes, but with a scattering of white people. A young girl with pale skin, dressed like any coed anywhere, in the clothes for a public occasion, is on the rostrum. She is leaning forward a little on her high heels, speaking with a peculiar vibrance in a strong irregular rhythm, out of some inner excitement, some furious, taunt élan, saying, '...and I tell you I have discovered a great truth. I have discovered a great joy. I have discovered that I am black. *I am black!* You out there—oh, yes, you may have black faces, but your hearts are white, your minds are white, you have been white-washed!' (Warren, 1966, p. 17).

Black writers probably represent as reliable an index as is available regarding the developing future of the new black self. From DuBois's (1903) classic statement on the inaudibility of blacks to the works of Baldwin (1961) and Ellison (1966) suggesting invisibility, namelessness, and facelessness, we can almost feel the determined demand of these creative men to be heard, to be seen, and to be recognized as selves, as *black* selves. There can be little doubt that such writers have been powerful movers among black Americans in their search for self. They have set the stage for the dramatic shift from a self characterized by a sense of nobodiness to a self soaked through with somebodiness; a change from a self that is mirrored against white significant others, to a self that is clearly and proudly reflecting black significant others.

With an increased orientation toward black significant others as the basis for self-evaluation, black consciousness has great potential for helping blacks attain self-realization and for helping them to overcome the strong negative self-imagery emanating from reflections in a white mirror. With the focus on black pride, the new black consciousness should do much toward the modification of the black self-image by encouraging black people to directly attack the questions of "what can we do for ourselves?" and "how can we overcome those elements in society that promote self-dissatisfaction and anxiety?" Black consciousness and black pride should be the catalysts for each individual to develop a self-concept that is appropriately assertive and that is continually in the process of actualization. Indeed, this is the type of self-concept that has always been most highly esteemed and rewarded in our society. Perhaps the most relevant and immediate goal for the development of the new black self has to be self-determination rather than self-realization. Surely, the self which is helpless in the face of economic, political, and social circumstances cannot be expected to allocate its energies entirely to actualization. Self-survival must precede self-realization, but one will never succeed without the other.

Black consciousness may also be an avenue by which black Americans can adjust to "competition shock," a potential source of anxiety to successfully striving black Americans. It has become possible for some black people to obtain the most coveted benefits of the American dream, benefits which exact a price that many black Americans will face in the future. Historically, blacks have had a built-in defense system to shield the self from many forms of failure. "What else can I do—that's all Whitey will let me have." "It's not my fault, a black man hasn't got a chance in a white world." This has been a primary defense for the black self, and very often a realistic one. Today, and in the not too distant future, it is a defense which will be increasingly unrealistic, however. When black failure can no longer automatically be blamed on the white majority but must come to rest on one's own inadequacies, it will require a strong and healthy self to adjust. Cobbs (1969) implores his black brothers and sisters to admit that "...there are no more psychological tricks blacks can play on themselves to make it possible to exist in dreadful circumstances. No more lies can they tell themselves. No more dreams to fix on. No more opiates to dull the pain...."

Hannery (1968) has described how the concept of "soul" in the urban black ghetto may, in part, be an attempt to overcome the ambivalence created by this situation. If a black person is unable to succeed, at least two alternatives are possible. First, it may be claimed that the achievement is impossible because of remaining social barriers based on prejudice. Second, it may be claimed that the achievement goal, although important according to the white majority, is not important according to soul standards. Hannery suggests that the concept of soul has been used to sum up alternative ideals and to provide a sense of solidarity and in-group security.

Recent research on the self-concept of blacks provides hard evidence supporting the notion that black consciousness not only is a security base for blacks facing a competitive society but also may promote the development of a positive self-image. The few early studies of the black self involved mostly elementary and junior high school pupils. These studies showed that white pupils had a more positive self-concept than did black pupils (Deutsch, 1960; Keller, 1963; Henton, 1964; Radke-Yarrow, 1965). More recent research, however, suggests that there is either no difference in the reported self-concepts of white and black children, or that black children have more positive self-concepts than white children (Zirkel & Moses, 1971; DeBlassie & Healy, 1970; Soares & Soares, 1969; Wilson, 1967).

Although an unambiguous explanation for this shift in self-concept is not available, it appears likely that it is largely a result of a bootstrap operation by black people rather than the result of economic and/or educational programs especially designed to produce such shifts. Research comparing the self-concepts of black pupils in integrated as compared with segregated school conditions, for example, has not generally indicated any effect on the reported self-concepts of black children due to school integration (Rohwer, 1971). In fact, the evidence tends to support the generalization that black children in segregated schools have a more positive self-concept (Coleman, 1966; Harootunian, 1968). Probably, the most important explanation lies in what has happened to the word *black* in the past few years. Black is now beautiful, and it is beautiful to be black. There has emerged a new feeling of pride in blackness and the distinctive characteristics of the black culture are manifested in black pride. It is important to emphasize that it has generally been only recently that studies have found more positive self-concepts for black children. The reporting of these research findings coincides with the development of the new black consciousness. Moreover, these outcomes support the predictions that can be made from Sullivan's theory regarding the influence on the black self due to the shift from predominantly white significant others to predominantly black significant others.

There is research evidence indicating that identification with the Movement has served to enhance the development of the new black self (Halpern, 1970; Roth, 1970). Related to the Movement, perhaps contributing substantially to it, is the unmeasured but obvious influence created by the new "black look" in the mass media (Colle, 1967). The rapidly increasing frequency with which blacks participate in local and network television drama, comedy, variety, news, and children's programs surely must present new black identification models for children and youth. Not only are black athletes and entertainers frequently seen on television and in the printed media, but also teachers, secretaries, doctors, attorneys, policemen, businessmen, politicians, fashion models and a widening range of possible occupational and social roles. Colle (1967) predicts that the potential of these new black role models to serve as significant others would be difficult to overestimate. It remains, however, for the specific aspects of the influence of television, movie, and magazine identification models on the black self to be scientifically documented.

The search of the black self for identity will go as it must. It will take many forms, some of which will turn out to be heartless hoaxes. Already, the black self may have suffered as much as it has gained as a result of some misguided aspects of the "black studies" movement. This widespread attempt, which peaked during the sixties, to create a past which could help blacks find an identity in the present was, in that respect, doomed to failure. Earlier separatist and escapist movements, like Father Divine's Heaven, and more nationalist movements, like Garvey's Universal Negro Improvement Association, provided rallying points in the black individual's search for self. Today, many liberated blacks look toward the Black Muslims and the Black Panthers as referents of racial solidarity, loyalty, and strength. These agencies can serve as sources of self-esteem for both members and non-members. Himes (1968), writing on the "identity functions of conflict," reminds readers that realistic racial conflict permits many blacks to accrue a considerable measure of identity within the American social system. He summarizes his argument thus:

> Intense alienation kept alive the Negro's quest for identity and meaning. Miraculously almost, realistic racial conflict with its ideological apparatus and action system functions to alleviate alienation and to facilitate identity. Conflict enhances group solidarity, clarifies group boundaries and strengthens the individual-group linkage through ego-emotion commitment and overt action. In-group identity is extended to the larger social system through the extension of communication, the enlargement of the network of social interactions and ideological devotion to national core values. It may be said, then, that through realistic racial conflict America gains some new Americans (Himes, 1968, p. 113).

Logically, the black church should serve an important identity function since it has the longest unbroken history of providing group cohesion. It appears, however, that the black church has, for the most part, been another form of escape from the realities of the black condition through its emphasis on fundamentalist doctrines and by encouraging emotional ventilation through its music and active participatory services. To be sure, there do exist happy exceptions. Among the more than 50,000 black churches represented by the five major black denominations with a combined membership of over ten million members, there are virtually no church-sponsored programs for community work with black youth, for adult education, health and cultural improvement, job training and placement. Young urban blacks appear to be rejecting the church as never before because they see them serving no meaningful purpose, and because they are controlled by "Toms." The church simply must provide more to the Movement than its music and a place to hold its meetings.

The Role of the School in the Future of the Black Self

At least two popular reports have recently joined those which take the position that schools bring little influence to bear on a child's achievement that is independent of his background and social context (Mosteller & Moynihan, 1972; Jencks et al., 1972). Both of these works are based primarily on thorough reanalyses of the Coleman Report (1966) data. Indeed, Coleman did conclude essentially that schools don't make a difference; family background determines student achievement. The methodological and conceptual problems which plagued the massive Coleman study* have been widely discussed by the experts but largely ignored by laymen and policy makers.

The Jencks et al. (1972) and the Bane and Jencks (1972) position is also based on a rehash of the Coleman Report plus data from Project Talent and the U.S. Census Bureau. These authors have prepared a brief for the argument that egalitarian school reforms, regardless of their size, scope, and intention, cannot make a substantial dent in the social inequality of adult Americans. Jencks and his colleagues suggest instead that school reformers should both lower and change their goals. They claim that reformers would be better advised to promise consumers only that new programs would make schools better and happier places for pupils and teachers to be. They further argue that achievement, so long the "holy grail" of educators, should give way to more affective and humanistic objectives. Nothing, they espouse, should be claimed regarding the likely positive effects of school programs on cognitive skills, achievement, IQ, or school equality since none of these factors has been found to play a meaningful part in increasing the life chances of pupils once they leave school. Finally, having summed up their

*1. The technique used to determine the social background of pupils is questionable. The determination was based solely on parent education without consideration of parent occupation and income.
2. The "no-school-effect" conclusion was based on a too narrowly defined criterion of school effectiveness.
3. Too few items were included on some tests to reliably measure important variables; in other instances, inappropriate tests were used, sometimes incorrectly.
4. There were flaws in the research design, including a biased sample.
5. The Report casts doubt on some of its findings by restricting, modifying, and even contradicting them.

case for the prosecution of public education (the charge: failure to overcome initial pupil differences), they conclude that adult equality in the U.S. can only be achieved by changing to a socialist form of government.

The potential influence of the Jencks et al. book (*Inequality*) must not be taken lightly as "simply another leftist, antischools, anti-Establishment attack." For openers, Jencks et al. conclude that even *good* schooling and *good* student performance have very little to do with children's future life chances. Further, they state their research shows that increasing expenditures on schools had very little to do with eliminating inequality. In fact, the ink on *Inequality* had scarcely dried when Jencks was accused (*Washington Post*, April 3, 1973) of providing the "pseudointellectual underpinnings" for the Supreme Court's refusal to order equal per-pupil expenditures in a Texas school finance case (handed down March 21, 1973). It may not have been by choice, but here is the unlikely situation of Jencks, a *very* liberal scholar, becoming the chief wrecking tool for a conservative administration bent on dismantling compensatory education, a cherished child of the liberal establishment.

There are a number of implications stemming from the Coleman/ Mosteller-Moynihan/Jencks reports which may impinge on the future of the black self. The first and, perhaps, most important implication is that these revisionist reports, particularly Jencks, have become the principal inspiration for the conservative perspective of the 1970s in much the fashion that Galbraith's (1958) *Affluent Society* was a primary manual for the Great Society of the 1960s. Galbraith declared that poverty is self-perpetuating because the poorest groups of Americans are poorest in the services that could eliminate it. By the end of the Sixties, when it became undeniably clear to all that the war on poverty wasn't pulling people out of poverty, the warriors fell back to another more defensible position—i.e., the claim that the war on poverty was actually pursuing a long-term strategy, equalizing opportunities by improving the poor—compensatory education, manpower training, health care, and community organization, all of which would pay off in the future.

Even this long-term strategy finally surrendered to the shelling administered by Jencks and the Harvard brigade. Daniel Patrick Moynihan, another member of the Harvard group, through his close association with the Executive Branch influenced the federal government to move away from the compensatory education strategy and toward a guaranteed income approach. *Inequality* appeared in mid-fall of 1972. Less than a year later, the Office of Economic Opportunity and most U.S. Office of Education compensatory programs were on their way out.

A second implication which affects the future sociopolitical climate of the black self has to do with the manner in which Jencks's conclusions have been applied. Asbury (1972) points out that Jencks and his consumers have confused the important difference between "equality of opportunity" as a goal and "making people equal." Asbury, a Howard University educational psychologist, says that the goal of compensatory education programs was not to *make pupils equal* and should, therefore, not be attacked for failure to do so. The goal of these programs was to *equalize the opportunity* for each pupil to fully realize his or her potential. The poverty programs should be criticized for the general failure to achieve the latter aim, not the former.

One of the ironies of the war on poverty is that in some ways it actually increased income inequalities by providing jobs and salaries for middle-class black and white poverty workers. As Moynihan (Mosteller & Moynihan, 1972) puts it, "The rewards to these individuals were substantial for they included the satisfaction of doing well while doing good" (p. 86).

Finally, and most directly related to the theme of *The Black Self,* the Jencks's conclusion that "the character of a school's output depends largely on. . . the characteristics of the entering children" ignores a set of factors not able to be included in *Inequality.* Broadly, this set of factors has to do with the fundamental changes occurring in many U.S. schools today. The major administrative, personnel, and architectural changes notwithstanding, there are some potentially dramatic changes taking place in the curriculum, the heart of the school, which have important implications for the black self. Several examples of such changes are described later in this chapter. Suffice it to say that the many attempts to bring the cognitive components of the school curriculum into a realistic balance with previously ignored affective learning factors (self-concept, sense of environmental control, sociopolitical attitudes) may, as Coleman (1966) concluded, have more to do with successful social adaptation of the black self than all the other school variables combined.

The intense disenchantment of black Americans with education at all levels is symptomatic of the deep dissatisfaction with society generally. Yet, blacks have zeroed in on the school because this institution is generally seen as a primary force for good in the life chances of their young. Right or wrong, the majority of *all* Americans view education as the one great hope for their children.

> The schools are crucial to any positive resolution of the problems of the ghetto. As long as these ghetto schools continue to turn out thousands and thousands of functional illiterates yearly, Negro youth will not be prepared for anything other than menial jobs or unemployment and dependency; they will continue the cycle of broken homes, unstable family life, and neglected and uneducated children. The tragic waste of human resources will go on unabated (Clark, 1970, p. 302).

The reader may be familiar with the commonly held assumption that black parents generally reject education and that they mediate this attitude to their children. After reviewing the research on the relationship between social class and school achievement, Brookover and Gottlieb (1963) concluded that black families place a high premium on education, despite their apparent inability (or unwillingness) to communicate these values to the white educational bureaucracy. Public education continues to be society's prime instrument for perpetuating its cultural heritage. The crucial question, which only future action can answer, is whether or not public education is willing to perpetuate a cultural heritage which is racially and socially realistic.

The Black Movement is trying to bring about change in public education by righting wrongs which have piled up over 300 years. Many of these efforts revolve around a vivid, effective renewal of our democratic commitment to educate *all* our children to their fullest social and intellectual potential and to do so without forcing black children to reject their ethnic identity and the unique qualities of their blackness. Although the school is unable to control the conditions out of which deep-seated reactions spring, it can make contributions toward the emergence of a black self less prone to self-defeating behaviors and interactions. It falls upon the school to provide the types of learning climates which will permit and encourage black children to alter their self-images, so that they desire and are able to achieve a level of competence that makes it possible for them to compete successfully in a modern industrial society. Concurrently, it must be possible for pupils to learn that racism is as much a white problem as it is a black problem (perhaps even more so a white problem). Cobbs (1969) has demanded that

> The educational process must be shifted in school, so that every class at every grade level will discuss feelings about race. We must make this nation one vast encounter group...all schools should devote an entire quarter to discussing nothing but race (p. 27).

The position espoused by Dr. Cobbs, a black man who is a psychiatrist, is one which has been implemented in some form by many U.S. schools as they attempt to desegregate. Human relations seminars, human relations fairs, human relations workshops, human relations consultants, human relations directors, and so on, buzz thickly around the honey of federal funds which has been poured over the bitterness of the school desegregation process. There simply are no trustworthy data available regarding the effects of these programs. Such efforts often imply that as soon as black and white pupils and teachers accept and understand one another, they can somehow get down to the nitty-gritty of education and learn efficiently and effectively. Time will tell.

Another position, more popular among educators and psychologists, is that the key lies in teaching young black children the *cognitive skills* required for success in school. Deutsch (1963) claims that the black child upon entering school is so poorly prepared to produce what the school demands that failure is almost inevitable. He suggests that stimulus deprivation, the condition of poverty, and inadequate training in auditory and visual discrimination are responsbile for the black child's handicaps. Riessman (1962) and Bernstein (1961) suggest that the black school child's deficits are *verbal* rather than *perceptual* as indicated by Deutsch. It has been documented by Riessman and by Bernstein that young black children do, indeed, use adjectives better than verbs: understand more language than they use; produce short, grammatically simple, often unfinished sentences with poor syntactical form; make little use of subordinate clauses; infrequently use impersonal pronouns; and so on.

Who is correct—Cobbs, who says the schools should do battle with feelings, attitudes, and emotions surrounding the black child in a white-controlled bureaucracy? Or are Deutsch, Riessman, and Bernstein right, representing, as they do, the forces who believe a frontal assault on the cognitive-learning deficits presented by the poor black child is the paramount responsibility of the educational enterprise? A brief perusal of any school curriculum or of most programs of professional teacher preparation quickly shows that American education has always been on the "cognitive deficits" path. Matters of the intellect have a tradition of measurability and precision in this society; matters of the heart do not. Attempts to adapt the school environment for poor black children have primarily been *cognitive* adaptations.

In the face of education's cognitive position, Zigler (1966, 1968) has presented an impressive body of research evidence showing that feelings about self (attitudinal, motivational, and emotional factors) depress school achievement and learning of disadvantaged black and white pupils below the level expected for their chronological ages. American education has failed to come to grips with this type of evidence largely because of the tendency to blame academic failures on flaws in the environment of black children. It is foolish to deny that poor urban and rural children are likely to be deprived of many of the experiences that facilitate school learning. It is equally foolish, however, to deny that schools in America have failed to develop a climate for learning which is geared to the needs of such children. It is tragically common for teachers to perceive their black pupils as being indifferent and unmotivated and to conclude that little can be done to educate them until positive changes are brought about in their family or environment. It only deepens the tragedy to find that many black teachers are among those holding such beliefs and expectations.

Racial Segregation or Social-Class Segregation?

When the term "segregation" is used in conjunction with education, it is assumed that the speaker is referring to racial segregation. Racial segregation has been defined *operationally:*

Schools whose student body is less than 10 percent Negro will be classified "white" segregated schools; if less than 10 percent of the student body is white, the schools will be considered "Negro" segregated schools; the remainder will be referred to as "integrated" schools (Hauser Report, 1964, p. 17).

Racial segregation has also been defined *psychologically:*

[Segregation] means that the personal worth, of either a white or Negro person, is measured solely by group membership regardless of individual merit. Such a measure is realistically false and of necessity distorts the developing self-image of Negro and white children as well as their view of each other. Under these psychological circumstances the Negro child, for example, is burdened with inescapable inferiority feelings, a fixed ceiling to his aspiration level which can constrict the development of his potentialities, and a sense of humiliation and resentment which can entail patterns of hatred against himself and his own group, as well as against the dominant white group (Bernard, 1958, p. 151).

Because of the controversy surrounding racial segregation, the important issue of social- and economic-class segregation has been largely ignored. Pettigrew (1972), well-known for his work on the personality of the black American, states that

Our schools are not quite, but almost, as socially class segregated in America today as they are racially segregated. We have evidence that strongly suggests— if it does not definitely prove—that for a lower-class child to go to a predominantly middle-class school does in fact improve his achievement over what it probably would have been if he had remained in a predominantly lower-class school (p. 55).

The implications of social-class segregation for the educational future of black children are interesting. First, it means that in order to be effective, future desegregation efforts will require not only a cross-section of children of all races but of all classes and economic groups. Second, it means that Americans who are uneasy about the concept of social class are going to be more uneasy when it becomes clear that providing equal educational opportunity is not a racial problem so much as it is a class problem. Third, poor blacks may find themselves joined by poor whites in their demand for educational opportunities for their children. Desegregation may produce more strange bedfellows than politics.

Compensatory Education and the Black Self

American consumers of public education can expect to see (and pay for) a greater number and variety of compensatory education programs in the future than they have already seen pass in review. The confused, tax-paying consumer has tended to lump compensatory, enrichment, and intervention programs together without being able to distinguish the "good" from the "bad." These massive, federally supported efforts have tended to be relatively unidentifiable one from another in the eyes of laymen. Americans are up to their wallets in such programs which are usually referred to by some meaningless number (Title I, Title III, Title VI, etc.) or by some clever acronym (HOPE, WAY, LIFE, FITE) or by a Madison Avenue title with "grab" and "clout" (Headstart, Upward Bound, Follow-Through). The great majority of these compensatory programs have taken the same "cognitive deficits" route discussed earlier in connection with public education. Most of the early childhood intervention programs report striking increases in IQ. For a long period of time, beginning with the Iowa Studies* in the late 1930s through the preschool studies of the 1960s, that seemed sufficient. The assumption appears to have been made that by stimulating cognitive growth in black and white lower class children, factors related to self-perception would also be positively enhanced.

It is true that, today, the young black self is not faced with the over-stringent, mechanical cognitive stimulation models of the past. However, more contemporary compensatory models must take great care not to accept the assumption that IQ rises and positive self-perceptions are necessarily related without rigorous testing.

More recent compensatory education efforts appear to be going somewhat beyond the usual lip service paid to affective factors. There are new attempts being made to provide learning environments which are specifically designed to help black children and youth develop positive self-attitudes and a meaningful self-realization.† Of equal importance is the increased interest in the systematic measurement of these self factors.

Critics of compensatory education have been many in number and varietous in their range of reason and scholarship. A position which can be disagreed with but should not be ignored is one presented by sociologists Farber and Lewis (1972). Despite the questionable nature of their interpretation of the assumptions which they claim to undergird compensatory education in America, Farber and Lewis view compensatory efforts as a manifestation of "progressive status-quoism." The self-contradiction inherent in the term is intentional. These authors define *progressive statusquoism* as

---

*Skeels, H., R. Updegraff, B. Wellman, & A. Williams. A study of environmental stimulation: An orphanage preschool project. *University of Iowa Studies in Child Welfare*, 1958, 15, No. 4; Skodak, M., & H. Skeels. A final follow-up study of one hundred adopted children. *Journal of Genetic Psychology*, 1949, 75, 85-125; Wellman, B. Iowa studies on the effects of schooling. *Yearbook of National Social Studies Education*, 1940, 39, 377-99.

†See, for example, the *Social Learning Curriculum* developed by Dr. Herbert Goldstein (1969) and his colleagues at Yeshiva University in New York. See also the comprehensive instructional package developed and distributed by American Guidance Service, Inc., Circle Pines, Minnesota, called DUSO (Developing an Understanding of Self and Others), 1971.

...a symbolic or apparent attack on a social problem, as opposed to a real attempt to deal with that problem. Such an attack does not adequately deal with the root causes of the problem and does little more than to foster the illusion that something is being done (we are making progress) when, in fact, nothing or, at best, very little is being accomplished (the status-quo is being maintained) (Farber & Lewis, 1972, p. 92).

Farber and Lewis maintain that progressive status-quoism is not a "conscious conspiracy" on the part of social scientists and educators against lower-class Americans. They suggest that compensatory programs are developed and implemented largely by professional educators who sincerely, but incorrectly, believe that such interventions can be effective. Farber and Lewis claim that compensatory education *cannot* be really effective because it rests on the "cognitive deficits" assumption. It is their position that the real causes of cognitive deficits are not to be found in disadvantaged, ghetto environments and life styles, but in the external constraints which others place upon the personal development and life chances of the poor.

Blacks Within the Educational Enterprise

One idea which should be given greater exposure and increased investigation is the development and expansion of career opportunities for blacks within the educational system. Unless recent protracted school boycotts and strikes involving black teachers and parents were isolated phenomena, similar confrontations can be anticipated in the future. It should be noted that these conflicts occurred in cities which have received massive federal aid to schools, much of it going for compensatory programs. Farber and Lewis (1972) advance the gloomy prediction that "...our persistence in the compensatory course and progressive status-quoism in general will lock us into a vicious cycle in which *mainstream America* and the *other America* become increasingly polarized in mutual antagonism and opposition" (p. 94). These sociologists are questioning how much longer compensatory education will keep the black self sufficiently tranquilized in its present state so that it will not bite the hand that feeds it welfare.

Pearl and Riessman (1965) have described U.S. schools as constituting a "colonial imposition" on poor blacks because the school represents one more establishment agency which caters only to white majority values and standards. Essentially nothing about the system has ever belonged to black people. These authors have developed the structure of a plan which would permit educators to join with currently disinherited Americans in cooperative, interactive efforts aimed at reducing the barriers to opportunity for the black self. They have suggested that the employment of the indigenous poor by schools to serve "meaningful" roles in the instructional program could be an important initial step toward producing a fundamental change in the character of our schools.

Pearl and Riessman are talking about more than the hiring of a few black women as aides in Headstart. Far too often, in fact, such black teacher aides have become teacher "maids." The proposal includes poor blacks becoming truly a part of the teaching organization by entering the system as aides and being encouraged to gain the professional training to move along the continuum serving as teaching assistants, teaching associates, teachers, and supervisors. This idea is not without its weaknesses, including the fact that the American educational enterprise has no experience at identifying, recruiting, and screening potential employees from the ghetto, not to mention their training and supervision. However, the Pittsburgh and Philadelphia boards of education experimented with apparent success in the employment of ghetto residents in their schools as long ago as the early 1960s.*

Gartner, Kohler, and Riessman (1972) have developed the nucleus of an effort which involves the use of ghetto children as teachers. The idea, popularly called "peer tutoring," is the type of simple, straightforward approach often overlooked because of the apparent feeling that complex problems can't have simple answers. These authors report that in a New York City antipoverty education program (Mobilization for Youth), a group of tutored pupils gained an average of six months in measured reading achievement over a period of five months. During the same period, their tutors gained an average of 3.4 years in reading achievement. This is not to suggest that educators should rush blindly into massive peer-tutoring programs without careful investigation, but neither should they automatically distrust a technique which is so administratively simple and so financially inexpensive.

The influence of ghetto programs on the gripping handicap of social and personal impotence is not yet known, even in broad terms. It must be discouraging, if not damaging, however, to young black children who seldom see blacks in teaching leadership positions and even more rarely in posts of administrative authority in their "integrated" schools. The plan described by Pearl and Riessman (1965) *could,* if permitted, allow blacks to assume responsibility and exert some measure of local control over schools which have ignored, victimized, or inadequately served them for generations. The plan appears on its surface to potentially combine the most positive aspects of black militancy on the one hand, and white-dominated federal aid on the other.

*Pittsburgh Board of Education, *Team Teaching Projects Reports,* 1960; Philadelphia Board of Education, *Great Cities School-Community Improvement Project Reports,* 1962-1963.

The Black Parent and the School

An approach which is certainly not new, but which has never been used or tested effectively on a wide scale, is parent involvement. An historical review of parent-teacher programs by Meyer (1962) indicates that some educational leaders advocated such cooperative relationships as early as the 1830s. More recently, a few school units have even created positions for the home teacher, school-community coordinator, visiting teacher, parent-education counselor, and so on. The development of the Parent-Teacher Association near the turn of the present century is yet another testimony to a general interest in school-parent cooperation. For lower-class black families, urban and rural, the history of parent attitudes toward school has been characterized by suspicion and rejection (Fusco, 1964); unpleasant memories of their own school experience (Marburger, 1963); seeing white teachers as belonging to a higher social class and looking down on black children (McNassor, 1954; NEA, 1962); and, the belief that school has no long-range value for their children (Niemeyer, 1962).

Almost no compensatory education program is without its "parent involvement" component. Yet, few substantive data are available which would permit objective conclusions as to their effectiveness and their influence on self-attitudes of poor children. Research evidence is available which shows that children of ghetto parents who participated in organized school-home programs made significantly greater gains in reading (Schiff, 1963) and arithmetic (Duncan, 1964) achievement than children of non-participating or marginally participating parents. In some cases, the so-called parent involvement efforts which are attached to education and poverty program grants are excellent examples of Farber's "status quoism" discussed earlier. Black parents are often recruited to serve on advisory committees and boards of directors of such projects in the apparent hope that these highly visible but essentially powerless appointments will meet granting requirements while keeping local residents happy or at least fooled. It would neatly fit the image which many blacks maintain of the white majority to report that these "rip-offs" are all perpetrated by Whitey, but alas, carpetbaggers have never been all white.

Once again, the relative contributions of social class and race to the school-parent situation are indistinguishable. Research data have indicated repeatedly over a period of twenty years that persons of low socioeconomic status participate significantly less in such formal voluntary organizations as the school than do persons of higher socioeconomic status (Mather, 1941; Dotson, 1951; Axelrod, 1956; Bell & Force, 1956; Foskett, 1959; and Greer & Kube, 1959). Rempson (1968), in an outstanding critical review of contemporary school-parent programs, concludes that

...there is no research evidence disclosing that school-parent programs in depressed urban neighborhoods have had any substantial success in themselves... in achieving either their immediate objectives or their ultimate goal. It would be surprising if, individually, the bulk of the programs has influenced more than 10 percent of the parents to improve the intellectual environment they provide for their children (pp. 143-144).

The Political Education of the Black Self

The future of America's schools has for at least twenty years been in the hands of the federal government. Perhaps this is not only necessary but desirable. This political and economic relationship can only grow closer as local and state resources fail to keep pace with school needs. The federalism of schools in particular and the federalism of community and urban life in general holds crucial implications for the future of the black self. As the educational planning and decision-making responsibility is moved further away from local citizens, the individual consumer of school services finds it increasingly difficult to influence the decisions made regarding the education of his children. This "political separation" is faced by all Americans, but it may be even more important for Americans who are also black. Potentially, for lower-class blacks, the increased political distance between them and the school may be more psychologically damaging than for middle-class blacks. The basic reason is their low sense of political efficacy.

Seasholes (1956) points out that blacks who do not participate politically differ from white nonparticipants in two important ways. First, proportionately fewer blacks participate in any form of political activity than whites. Second, and undoubtedly related to the first reason, is that blacks have "real or imagined fears of reprisal, ranging from physical violence to economic reprisal or even just personal insult..." (Seasholes, 1965, p. 66). Seasholes makes an important distinction between the black self which rejects political participation because of the belief that politics is a white, racist conspiracy, from the black self which believes that political impotence is only an extension of self-impotence. In the latter case, the paternalistic nature of federally supported school and community programs may simply reinforce his belief that he has no personal control, thereby either widening or solidifying the psychological separation between him and his ability to influence the quality of his own child's education. The more external support this black self receives without his political participation, the more convinced he becomes that, internally, he has no personal control over what happens to his children, educationally. How is the sense of personal control influenced when blacks see that school, neighborhood, and community programs are provided without their even asking for them (for some, without their ever thinking about them)?

Most black activists are intensely aware that the only realistic answers to urban and rural ghetto problems lie in political activity. Even Stokely Carmichael, who has frightened America with his angry and revolutionary rhetoric, sees political involvement as the heart of black power.

> Black power is a call for black people in this country to unite, to recognize their heritage, to build a sense of community...Group solidarity is necessary before a group can operate effectively in a pluralistic society (Carmichael & Hamilton, 1967, p. 44).

In an interview conducted by Gordon Parks (1967) for *Life* magazine, Carmichael again expressed his ideas about the real meaning of black power:

> Black power doesn't mean anti-white, violence, separatism, or any other racist things the press says it means. It's saying, "Look buddy, we're not laying a vote on you unless you lay schools, hospitals, playgrounds, and jobs on us."

Regardless of the influence and the wisdom developed by leaders of the Movement concerning the importance of political involvement, the black self will not rise to the call of politics, because it cannot. It cannot because of the overwhelming feeling of self-impotence, and because it has never been taught to use the tools of politics. Obviously, these factors are closely tied together.

It is curious that the school which is a politically determined institution has nearly always taught political *concepts,* but has never taught the *skills* of political behavior. Of course, those who have been academically successful have been the ones who have been able to translate abstract political concepts into realistic political action. It is a responsibility of parents, family, church, and social groups to teach positive political attitudes and to encourage the political socialization of children. Whether or not a child's extraschool environment discharges this responsibility, the school must accept a primary role for political socialization of America's young. The process should begin as early as possible in the child's school career. Grambs (1968) has developed an excellent set of curriculum resources which is designed to actively engage pupils of all ages in the acquisition of attitudes and skills which underlie political effectiveness. Weinstein and Fantini (1970) have developed and successfully used a "curriculum of affect" designed to deal realistically and directly with the self-factors which are pre-requisites to a belief in political self-adequacy.

Richmond's (1972) ideas concerning classrooms as "microeconomies" developed in the Society School on Manhattan's Lower East Side, contain great potential for ghetto pupils. It is Richmond's belief that contemporary schools fail to meet the test of relevance because they focus on the *abstract* rather than the *actual* workings of the sociopolitical system.

Society Schooling is based on the premise that human beings actualize themselves through work, that positive self-concepts are formed as individuals respond positively and successfully to stimuli in their immediate environment, and that learning to initiate, to lead, and to organize work is a vital form of education (p. 45).

Others have begun to explore the values of fostering learning environments in which pupils create miniature societies. The Parkway School in Philadelphia (Bremer & von Moschzisker, 1971) has attempted to integrate secondary school learning with other ongoing societal institutions. The Frank Porter Graham Child Development Center, in Chapel Hill, North Carolina, is developing outstanding elementary-level micro-organizations which parallel existing organizations in the adult community.

Approaches such as these permit the creative blending of cognitive learning with pupils' feelings and attitudes about how such learning relates to their life chances and teaches that these cognitive skills are means to survival, not boring, detached ends in themselves. As more psychologists and educators turn their attention to the translation of variables related to self-learning and the acquisition of political skills into meaningful instructional packages, the life chances of the black self can but improve. The following statement by Seasholes (1965) spells out in unequivocal language the role of the public school in the political socialization of the black self:

> While there is much other than what happens to Negroes in school that puts them at a political disadvantage, this fact should not deter us from trying to maximize the impact the school experience can have on their later political effectiveness... Perhaps the greatest contribution we as educators could make to the school-age Negroes who will be tomorrow's adult citizens is to reorient their thinking (and incidentally, our own) about the development and use of political strategy. This means spelling out with approval the various techniques of bargaining, forced demands, concession, and occasional retreat that are used by politically successful subgroups in our society.... It means being candid on two scores when dealing with heterogeneous groups of students in the classroom—candid about the probable maximum of political potential that a given subgroup could have (just how successful Negroes can expect to be, given their total resources of numbers, money, effort, education, and so forth), and candid about the kinds of political techniques that are in fact being used currently or may be used in the reasonably near future (p. 67).

The present chapter has suggested that American education will be expected to serve a major role in the future of the black self. The school has traditionally been considered an apolitical institution, perhaps because one of its primary functions is that of a stabilizer or perpetuator of the society. The natural instability of politics may not have been seen as conducive to that function. But, it must be remembered that the school has a second major function, and that is as an *agent of change*. Havighurst (1957), in his discussion of how education changes society, says that, "As an agent of change, education acts under the direction of technological or ideological forces to make each generation different from its parents" (p. 86).

It is in the school's expression of its "agent of change" function that the greatest hopes for the future of the new black self reside.

References

Advisory Panel on Integration of the Public Schools ("The Hauser Report"). *Report to the Board of Education, City of Chicago.* Chicago: Board of Education, 1964.

Asbury, C. A. "Yesterday's failure." *Washington Post.* Sunday, October 15, 1972.

Axelrod, M. Urban structure and social participation. *American Sociological Review,* 1956, 21, 13-19.

Baldwin, J. *Nobody knows my name.* New York: The Dial Press, Inc., 1961.

Bane, M., & C. Jencks. The schools and equal opportunity. *Saturday Review* (October), 1972, 37-42.

Bell, W., & M. Force. Urban neighborhood types and participation in formal association. *American Sociological Review,* 1956, 21, 25-34.

Bernard, V. School desegregation: Some psychiatric implications. *Psychiatry,* 1958, 21, 149-58.

Bernstein, B. Social structure, language, and learning. *Educational Research,* 1961, 3, 168-76.

Bremer, J., & M. von Moschzisker. *School without walls.* New York: Holt, Rinehart, & Winston, 1971.

Broderick, F., & A. Meier, eds. *Negro protest thought in the twentieth century.* Indianapolis: Bobbs-Merrill, 1965.

Brookover, W., & D. Gottlieb. Social class and education. In W. Charter and N. Gage (eds.), *Readings in the social psychology of education.* Boston: Allyn & Bacon, 1963.

Bruner, J. *On knowing: Essays for the left hand.* Cambridge, Mass.: Harvard University Press, 1963.

Carmichael, S., & C. Hamilton. *Black power: The politics of liberation in America.* New York: Random House, 1967.

Clark, K. Ghetto schools: Separate and unequal. In R. Endo and W. Strawbridge (eds.), *Perspectives on black America.* Englewood Cliffs, N.J.: Prentice-Hall, 1970.

Cobbs, P. Speech given at 53rd annual convention of the National Association of School Principals, 1969.

Coleman, J., et al. *Equality of educational opportunity.* Washington, D.C.: U.S. Government Printing Office, 1966.

Colle, R. The Negro image and the mass media. Unpublished doctoral dissertation, Cornell University, 1967. (Dissertation Abstracts, 1968, 28, 309A-310A)

DeBlaissie, R., & G. Healy. Self-concept: A comparison of Spanish-American, Negro, and Anglo adolescents across ethnic, sex, and socioeconomic variables. Las

Cruces, N.M.: ERIC Clearinghouse on Rural Education and Small Schools, 1970.

Dentler, R., et al., eds. *The urban r's.* New York: Praeger, 1968.

Deutsch, M. The disadvantaged child and the learning process. In A. Passow (ed.), *Education in depressed areas.* New York: Teachers College, Columbia University Press, 1963.

Deutsch, M. *University group and class status as related to social and personality factors in scholastic achievement.* Ithaca, N.Y.: Cornell University Press, 1960.

Dotson, F. Patterns of voluntary association among urban working-class families. *American Sociological Review,* 1951, 16, 687-93.

DuBois, W. *The souls of black folk.* Chicago: A. C. McClurg, 1903.

Duncan, R. An experimental study of the effect of parents' knowledge on student performance in SMSG mathematics. *Journal of Educational Research,* 1964, 58, 135-37.

Ellis, N., ed. *International review of research in mental retardation.* Vol. 1. New York: Academic, 1966.

Ellison, R. *Shadow and act.* New York: Random House, 1966.

Endo, R., & W. Strawbridge, eds. *Perspectives on black America.* Englewood Cliffs, N.J.: Prentice-Hall, 1970.

Farber, B., & M. Lewis. Compensatory education and social justice. *Peabody Journal of Education,* 1972, 49, 85-96.

Foskett, J. The influence of social participation on community programs and activities. In M. Sussman (ed.), *Community structure and analysis.* New York: Thomas Y. Crowell, 1959.

Fusco, G. School-home partnership in depressed urban areas. Office of Education Bulletin No. 20. Washington, D.C.: U.S. Government Printing Office, 1964.

Galbraith, J. K. *The affluent society.* Boston: Houghton-Mifflin, 1958.

Gartner, A., M. Kohler, & F. Riessman. *Children teach children.* New York: Harper & Row, 1972.

Grambs, J. *Intergroup education: Methods and materials.* Englewood Cliffs, N.J.: Prentice-Hall, 1968.

Greer, S., & E. Kube. Urbanism and social structure. In M. Sussman (ed.), *Community structure and analysis.*

Halpern, F. Self-perception of black children in the civil rights movement. *American Journal of Orthopsychiatry,* 1970, 40, 520-26.

Hamachek, D., ed. *The self in growth, teaching, and learning.* Englewood Cliffs, N.J.: Prentice-Hall, 1965.

Hannery, U. The rhetoric of soul: Identification in Negro society. *Race,* 1968, 4, 453-65.

Harootunian, B. Self-other relationships of segregated and desegregated ninth graders. Paper presented at the annual meeting of the American Educational Research Association, Chicago, 1968. ERIC:ED 023 765.

Havighurst, R. How education changes society. *Confluence: An Educational Forum.* Spring, 1957, p. 86.

Henton, P. Relationships between the self-concepts of Negro elementary school children and their academic achievement, intelligence, interests and manifest anxiety. ERIC:ED 003 288.

Himes, J. The functions of racial conflict. In R. Mack (ed.), *Race, class, and power* (2nd ed.). New York: American Book, 1968.

Jencks, C., M. Smith, H. Acland, M. Bane, D. Cohen, H. Gintis, B. Heyns, & S. Michelson. *Inequality: A reassessment of the effect of family and schooling in America.* New York: Basic Books, 1972.

Keller, S. The social world of the urban slum child: Some preliminary findings. *American Journal of Orthopsychiatry,* 1963, 33, 823-31.

Kvaraceus, W., et al., eds. *Negro self-concept: implications for school and citizenship.* Englewood Cliffs, N.J.: Prentice-Hall, 1965.

Mack, R., ed. *Race, class, and power,* 2nd ed. New York: American Book, 1968.

Malcolm X. *The autobiography of Malcolm X.* New York: Grove Press, 1965.

Marburger, C. Considerations for educational planning. In A. Passow (ed.), *Education in depressed areas.*

Mather, W. Income and social participation. *American Sociological Review,* 1941, 6, 380-84.

McNassor, D. Barriers and gateways in school-community relationships. *Journal of Educational Sociology,* 1954, 28, 1-10.

Mead, G. *Mind, self, and society.* Chicago: University of Chicago Press, 1934.

Meyer, M. Parent-teacher relationships in the early nineteenth century. *Journal of Educational Research,* 1962, 56, 48-50.

Mosteller, F., & D. Moynihan, eds. *On equality of educational opportunity.* New York: Random House, 1972.

National Education Association and the American Association of School Administrators, *Education and the disadvantaged American.* Washington, D.C.: NEA, 1962.

Niemeyer, J. Home-school interaction in relation to learning in the elementary school. Paper presented at the Symposium on School Dropouts, held in Washington, D. C., sponsored by the National Education Association, 1962.

Parks, G. Stokely Carmichael: Young man behind an angry message, *Life,* May 19, 1967.

Passow, A., ed. *Education in depressed areas.* New York: Teachers College, Columbia University Press, 1963.

Pearl, A., & F. Riessman. *New careers for the poor.* New York: Free Press, 1965.

Pettigrew, T. Quote taken from, "The Duluth Experience," an article written by Dick Hubert, *Saturday Review,* May 27, 1972.

Philadelphia Board of Education, *Team teaching projects reports,* 1960.

Radke-Yarrow, M., et al. Social perceptions and attitudes of children. In D. Hamachek (ed.), *The self in growth, teaching, and learning.*

Rempson, J. School-parent programs in depressed urban areas. In R. Dentler, et al. (eds.), *The urban r's.*

Richmond, G. The "society school": An alternative to the deschooled society. *Saturday Review,* June 24, 1972.

Riessman, F. *The culturally deprived child.* New York: Harper & Row, 1962.

Rohwer, W. Learning, race, and school success. *American Educational Research Journal,* 1971, 41, 191-210.

Roth, R. How Negro fifth grade students view "black pride" concepts. *Integrated Education,* 1970, 8, 24-27.

Rustin, B. From protest to politics. In F. Broderick & A. Meier (eds.), *Negro protest thought in the twentieth century.*

Schiff, H. The effort of personal contractual relationships on parents' attitudes toward and participation in local school affairs. Unpublished doctoral dissertation. Evanston, Ill.: Northwestern University, 1963.

Seasholes, B. Political socialization of Negroes: Image development of self and polity. In W. Kvaraceus, et al. (eds.), *Negro self-concept: implications for school and citizenship.*

Skeels, H., R. Updegraff, B. Wellman, & A. Williams. A study of environmental stimulation: An orphanage preschool project. *University of Iowa Studies in Child Welfare,* 1958, 15, No. 4.

Skodak, M., & H. Skeels. A final follow-up study of one hundred adopted children. *Journal of Genetic Psychology,* 1949, 75, 85-125.

Soares, A., & L. Soares. Self-perceptions of culturally disadvantaged children. *American Educational Research Journal,* 1969, 6, 31-45.

Sullivan, H. *The interpersonal theory of psychiatry.* New York: Norton, 1953.

Sussman, M., ed. *Community structure and analysis.* New York: Thomas Y. Crowell, 1959.

Warren, R. *Who speaks for the Negro?* New York: Random House, 1966.

Weinstein, G., & M. Fantini. *Toward Humanistic Education: A curriculum of affect.* New York: Praeger, 1970 (Sponsored by the Ford Foundation).

Wellman, B. Iowa studies on the effects of schooling. *Yearbook of National Social Studies Education,* 1940, 39, 377-99.

Wilson, A. Educational consequences of segregation in a California community. In *Racial isolation in the public schools: A report of the U. S. Commission on Civil Rights.* Washington, D.C.: U.S. Government Printing Office, 1967.

Zigler, E., & E. Butterfield. Motivational aspects of IQ test performance of culturally deprived nursery school children. *Child Development,* 1968, 39, 1-14.

Zigler, E. Research on personality structure in the retardate. In N. Ellis (ed.), *International review of research in mental retardation* Vol. 1.

Zirkel, P., & E. Moses. Self-concept and ethnic group membership among public school students. *American Educational Research Journal,* 1971, 8, 253-65.

index